TASKS
AND
COMMUNICATING
IN
LANGUAGE
CLASSROOMS

The McGraw-Hill Second Language Professional Series

(FORMERLY "THE MCGRAW-HILL FOREIGN LANGUAGE PROFESSIONAL SERIES")

General Editors: James F. Lee and Bill VanPatten

Directions in Second Language Learning

(FORMERLY "DIRECTIONS FOR LANGUAGE LEARNING AND TEACHING")

Primarily for students of second language acquisition and teaching, curriculum developers, and teacher educators, *Directions in Second Language Learning* explores how languages are learned and used and how knowledge about language acquisition and use informs language teaching. The books in this strand emphasize principled approaches to language classroom instruction and management as well as to the education of foreign and second language teachers.

Tasks and Communicating in Language Classrooms
by James F. Lee (Indiana University)
Order number: 0-07-231054-5

Affect in Foreign Language and Second Language Learning: A Practical Guide to Creating a Low-Anxiety Classroom Atmosphere
Edited by Dolly Jesusita Young (The University of Tennessee)
Order number: 0-07-038900-4

Communicative Competence: Theory and Classroom Practice, Second Edition
by Sandra J. Savignon (The Pennsylvania State University)
Order number: 0-07-083736-8

Beyond Methods: Components of Second Language Teacher Education
Edited by Kathleen Bardovi-Harlig and Beverly Hartford (both of Indiana University)
Order number: 0-07-006106-8

Making Communicative Language Teaching Happen
by James F. Lee (Indiana University) and Bill VanPatten (University of Illinois, Urbana-Champaign)
Order number: 0-07-037693-X

Workbook to accompany *Making Communicative Language Teaching Happen*
by James F. Lee and Bill VanPatten
Order number: 0-07-037694-8

Perspectives on Theory and Research

Primarily for scholars and researchers of second language acquisition and teaching, *Perspectives on Theory and Research* seeks to advance knowledge about the nature of language learning in and out of the classroom by offering current research on language learning and teaching from diverse perspectives and frameworks.

Breaking Tradition: An Exploration of the Historical Relationship between Theory and Practice in Second Language Teaching
by Diane Musumeci (University of Illinois, Urbana-Champaign)
Order number: 0-07-044394-7

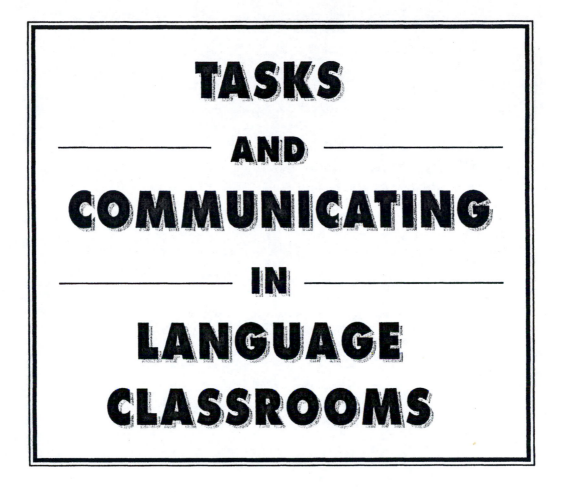

TASKS
AND
IN
LANGUAGE
CLASSROOMS

James F. Lee
Indiana University

Boston   Burr Ridge, IL   Dubuque, IA   Madison, WI   New York   San Francisco   St. Louis
Bangkok Bogotá Caracas Lisbon London Madrid
Mexico City Milan New Delhi Seoul Singapore Sydney Taipei Toronto

McGraw-Hill Higher Education

*A Division of The **McGraw-Hill** Companies*

This is an  book.

Tasks and Communicating in Language Classrooms

67890 QSR QSR 098765

ISBN 0-07-231054-5

Editor-in-chief: *Thalia Dorwick*
Senior sponsoring editor: *William R. Glass*
Senior development editor: *Becka McGuire*
Senior marketing manager: *Karen W. Black*
Project manager: *Beatrice Wikander*
Senior production supervisor: *Richard DeVitto*
Designer: *Suzanne Montazer*
Cover designer: *Carol Barr*
Editorial assistant: *Karen Privitt*
Compositor: *Shepherd, Inc.*
Typeface: *Palatino*

Library of Congress Cataloging-in-Publication Data
Lee, James F.
    Tasks and communicating in language classrooms / James F. Lee.
        p. cm.
    Includes index.
    ISBN 0-07-231054-5 (alk. paper)
    1. Languages, Modern--Study and teaching.   2. Communication in
education.   I. Title.
PB35.L428   2000
418′.007--dc21
                             99-30902
                             CIP

http://www.mhhe.com

Dedication

When my sister-in-law read the dedication to *Making Communicative Language Teaching Happen*, the book Bill VanPatten and I wrote, she scoffed at the fact that we had, in part, dedicated the book to our dogs. She asked why I hadn't dedicated the book to my parents. So here is a dedication to my parents, Ed and Mary Lee. I am eternally grateful for the sacrifices they made to send me to Putnam Catholic Academy, where I discovered Spanish. I would also like to dedicate this book to the memory of Juanita Pérez Trujillo VanPatten Mason. I lovingly called her my mother-in-law all those many years. And to Murphy, who is pretty good company, for a cat.

CONTENTS

FOREWORD

Communicative language teaching has evolved considerably since Sandra J. Savignon's contemporary inception of it in 1972. No longer seen simply as a matter of "personalizing the material" and somehow "getting students to talk," communicative language teaching has availed itself of a number of constructs that imply both structure and goal, for example: role play, Total Physical Response (TPR), content learning, immersion, processing writing, and interactive reading. Of increasing interest to curriculum developers, language teachers, and classroom researchers is the notion of *task*. Task type has shown to be a significant factor affecting the quality and quantity of communicative interaction among learners and teachers in the language classroom (e.g., Crookes & Gass 1993; Gass & Crookes 1993; Skehan 1997). In the present volume, James F. Lee offers a unique perspective on the development of tasks for the language classroom. He also provides empirical support of how the type of tasks he outlines affects communication in the classroom.

James F. Lee has long been known for his contribution to two areas: second language reading research, and communicative language teaching and curriculum development. In this book, he brings his expertise and experience from the latter to bear on one of the basic riddles for instructors-in-training and a good number of practicing instructors: How do we get learners to interact in meaningful ways using the "standardized" materials provided to us by our programs? Lee demonstrates how one can take the basic question-and-answer paradigm found in many, if not most, language textbooks and reformulate it into interactive tasks that place communication in the hands of the student-learners. His elegant framework of *framing, execution,* and *conclusion* offers a much-needed structure for developing tasks without tasking the instructor. At the same time, the framework demonstrates how tasks are goal- or outcome-oriented. While being practical and offering much in terms of task development and task-based test development, Lee's work is well grounded in theory and research. In Chapter 4 he describes one experiment in which he contrasts class discussion (led by the instructor) with an interactive task (led largely by the students). Interestingly, he shows that students talked significantly more (and better) when performing the task. In addition, he shows that students re-member more content (information) later on after having engaged in tasks rather than in discussion. In Chapter 7, Lee discusses tasks vis-à-vis current models of communicative competence and language ability, explaining just which aspects of competence tasks promote and those they may not.

Continuing in the tradition of bringing theory, research, and practice to-gether into one volume, Lee's volume is a welcome addition to the McGraw-Hill Second Language Professional Series. It will no doubt find a home on the shelves of many program directors, materials developers, instructors, and stu-dents of language education.

bvp
Champaign, Illinois

PREFACE

When I began studying Spanish in high school, we relied heavily on dialogue memorization and pattern practices. When I began teaching Spanish as a graduate student, we adhered to the curricular sequence: mechanical pattern drills to communicative drills to communicative practices. Then I met Tracy Terrell and learned about the Natural Approach. With time, experience, and exposure to others, my ideas on language teaching evolved. My ideas were informed by research on second language acquisition, classroom dynamics, and my work as director of large Spanish language programs. My own teaching has shifted considerably from its starting point, but the developments have been principled. We have heard and read much discussion concerning the role of negotiation in second language development. The emphasis on negotiation has brought attention to developing materials that privilege the kind of in-class interaction that maximizes learners' opportunities to negotiate meaning. In Chapter 1, I provide a definition of communication that guides the development of the rest of work. I also address the question, Why emphasize negotiation? What is the rationale for the professional interest in this type of communicative interaction? As the excerpts in Chapter 2 demonstrate, negotiated exchanges do not characterize all communicative classrooms.

The principal means by which learners can be provided these opportunities to negotiate meaning is through task-based activities. As I demonstrate in Chapter 3, many definitions of *task* exist. I therefore propose a consensus definition and then outline a principled approach to task-based instruction. In Chapter 3 I develop a set of activities that form the basis for developing all subsequent activities and test sections presented in the book. My decision to build on only a small set of activities was a purposeful one: These activities will be developed for non-beginners (Chapter 6), as in-class exam sections (Chapter 8), and as oral exam formats (Chapter 9). Although it might seem redundant, the reader will be able to make connections more easily as a result of seeing the activities develop.

In Chapter 4 I report the results of an experiment in communication that I conducted. I contrast a teacher-fronted question-and-answer format to communication with a task-based format. I present the results on participation patterns and information recalled as a result of the interactions. Not only do I present a principled approach to creating task-based materials, I also present a principled approach to implementing them (Chapter 5). I examine the activities via three points of encounter: framing the activity, executing it, and concluding it. I also pay great attention to the issue of time constraints. In the original draft of this chapter, I had presented the suggestions for implementing the activities in an expository prose format. In revising the manuscript I decided on a more narrative approach, in that I scripted words I would use if I were teaching the activities. I utilize this technique again in Chapter 6 for the section on implementing interaction at higher (non-beginner) levels of instruction.

In Chapter 7 I explore some of the issues surrounding the role of tasks in building language competence. I purposefully frame the discussion in broad terms (i.e., language competence) and not in terms of grammatical competence. This reflects my belief that language learning is far more than just learning the grammar of a language.

I am not unique in believing that until instructors alter their beliefs about testing, very little will change in the classroom. I have, therefore, written two chapters on language testing. In Chapter 8 I present suggestions for linking in-class, task-based activities to test sections. I propose two types of test sections: those that privilege the specific information resulting from the task-based activity and those that mirror the mental processes underlying the task-based activity. Finally, in Chapter 9, I demonstrate a task-based approach to oral testing. Transcripts of actual first-semester and fourth-semester learners carrying out task-based oral tests are presented and analyzed.

In addition to these two transcripts, the book contains several other examples of in-class interaction. Three interactions presented in Chapter 1 demonstrate various aspects of theories of acquisition and classroom practices. The heart of Chapter 2 consists of six excerpts from three different language classes. Chapter 4 presents the results of an experiment on communication, and transcripts are provided of the question-and-answer session and the task-based interaction. The instructors' decisions regarding how to manage the interaction are analyzed in Chapter 5. And, as previously mentioned, Chapter 9 contains transcripts of first- and fourth-semester learners carrying out the same oral test activity.

Rounding out each chapter in the book is a summary of the information presented, and then two practical sections, Gaining Greater Perspective and Application Activities. Gaining Greater Perspective provides a list of sources learners can consult for more information on topics developed in the chapter. In the Application Activities section, learners have the opportunity to use what they have learned in hands-on activities.

Acknowledgements

I wish to thank Bill VanPatten (University of Illinois, Urbana-Champaign) for his help in developing this work, talking to me about it, supporting it and me, and helping get it to publication. Many people have read and commented on early versions of this work and I am grateful for their feedback: Terry Ballman

(Western Carolina University), Carl Blyth (University of Texas at Austin), Rodney Bransdorfer (Central Washington University), Frank B. Brooks (Florida State University), Celeste Kinginger (The Pennsylvania State University), Gail Riley (Catholic University), Dolly Young (University of Tennessee, Knoxville), and William R. Glass (The Pennsylvania State University). I hope I haven't forgotten anyone. I have been teaching from manuscript versions of this book for several years and would like to acknowledge the many students (both graduate and undergraduate) who pushed me to clarify my thinking and my prose.

I also appreciate the insights of those who reviewed this work. They may or may not agree with the content, but their insights were helpful in shaping the work.

Marva Barnett (University of Virginia)
Heidi Byrnes (Georgetown University)
Graham Crookes (University of Hawai'i)
John Fanselow (Teachers College of Columbia University)
L. Kathy Heilenman (University of Iowa)
Janet Swaffar (University of Texas at Austin)

Finally, my thanks to the people at McGraw-Hill who helped make this work possible: Becka McGuire, Gregory Trauth, William R. Glass, Thalia Dorwick, and Beatrice Wikander.

James F. Lee
Indiana University

CHAPTER 1

Communication and Negotiation

CHAPTER OVERVIEW

Two ideas critical to any discussion of classroom language learning and teaching are *communication* and *negotiation*. The purpose of this chapter is to explore these concepts. First, we present certain tenets and practices associated with Audiolingual Methodology, a methodology that dominated language teaching during the post-war Baby Boom era and into the 1970s. An interesting connection between audiolingual practices and communicative practices will be made. The point will be made that contemporary communicative practices evolved from audiolingual practices. Another important point we will make in this chapter is that communication need *not* be equated with an instructor asking questions and learners answering them. Rather, communication will be defined as the *expression, interpretation, and negotiation of meaning*. This definition motivates the central question explored in this chapter: Why emphasize negotiation? Why do both second language researchers and teachers underscore the importance of negotiation in language classrooms?

WHAT IS COMMUNICATION?

The Second World War provided a need for military personnel proficient in multiple languages. The launching of a Russian satellite in 1957 created a sense of urgency regarding isolation from scientific advances made outside the United States. The intersection of language teaching with world politics, linguistics, and psychology led to an approach to structuring materials and classroom interaction termed *Audiolingual Methodology* (ALM) or *Audiolingualism*. The intent of this section is not to offer a history of language teaching, but simply to make some links with the recent past.

According to behaviorist psychology, all learning—verbal and nonverbal—takes place through the process of habit formation. Habits are formed through repetition and imitation of the language in the learner's environment. In Audiolingual Methodology, the language in the environment consisted of dialogues to be memorized and pattern practices or drills to be performed. Second language acquisition was seen to be the replacement of first language habits by second language habits. The first language, therefore, interfered with the acquisition of the second language. Maximum care was taken not to allow learners to make errors when producing the second language because errors were evidence of bad habits. "Audiolingualism (the term was coined by Professor Nelson Brooks in 1964) claimed to have transformed language teaching from an art to a science" (Richards & Rogers 1986, p. 48).

The shift from ALM to more communicatively oriented language instruction was a rather gentle one, representing more an evolution in instructional practices than a revolution of thought accompanied by a reexamination of practice. A case in point is Savignon's 1972 study comparing the effects of communicative practices with grammar-oriented ones. The experimental communicatively oriented instruction did not replace instruction and practice in grammar, but was carried out as a fifth day of instruction that replaced the laboratory component. All groups in the study received the same four days of traditional grammar or form-oriented instruction. The communication group outperformed the form-oriented group on two measures of communication; they performed just as well as the form-oriented group on measures of listening and reading comprehension (Savignon 1972, reprinted in Savignon 1997).

Although altering the laboratory component was hardly a revolution in thought or practice, the change did mark an important evolution in language teaching, and, in that sense, we witnessed an innovation in the development of contemporary language instruction. The idea that communication could and should take place in the classroom became more and more popular, due in part to research findings such as Savignon's. With changes in practice came changes in roles and responsibilities. The role of the language instructor was no longer supposed to be that of the drill leader. Instead, the instructor was charged with providing language learners opportunities for communication, that is, opportunities to use the language in contexts other than memorized dialogues and pattern practices. Insofar as communicative language teaching was a new construct to many instructors and not a well defined one, individuals were left to their own interpretations of what it meant to teach in a communicatively oriented framework. Two classroom practices became widely used: communicative drills and class discussions. Each of these classroom activities was firmly rooted in audiolingual instruction. The communicative drill was, however, no more than an extension (evolution) of the mechanical, structural drill that characterized so much of audiolingual practice (see Paulston 1978 for a classification of drills). Exercises 1 and 2 exemplify this evolution. The underlying purpose of both exercises is to practice irregular past-tense verbs in very controlled contexts, controlled so that learners make no errors that could lead them to form bad habits. Exercise 1 is an audiolingual drill, whereas Exercise 2 is its "communicative" counterpart of personalized questions.

Exercise 1. Substitution Drill

Your teacher will say a sentence. Substitute the past tense for the present.

INSTRUCTOR SAYS:	LEARNER RESPONDS:
1. I go to the movies.	1. I went to the movies.
2. I eat fish.	2. I ate fish.
3. I buy lunch.	3. I bought lunch.

Exercise 2. Communicative Drill

Answer with complete sentences the questions your teacher asks.

INSTRUCTOR SAYS:
1. Did you go to the movies last night?
2. Did you eat fish yesterday?
3. Did you buy lunch yesterday?

Two more examples serve to underscore the point that many communicative practices were firmly rooted in principles derived from structural linguistic thought underlying Audiolingual Methodology. Exercise 3 is a typical pattern-practice exercise characteristic of this methodology.

Exercise 3. Pattern Practice: Answering Negatively

Answer the questions your teacher asks according to the following model.

MODEL: Did you sleep well last night? → No, I did not sleep well last night.

INSTRUCTOR ASKS:
1. Did they study in the library last night?
2. Did she watch TV last night?
3. Did your friends go out to eat last night?

Exercise 4 represents the communicative counterpart of Exercise 3 in that learners ask each other questions. Of importance, from a communicative perspective, they are not directed to answer affirmatively or negatively but to answer truthfully.

Exercise 4. Communicative Drill

Your partner will ask you if you did the following things last night. Be sure to answer in complete sentences.

1. study in the library   2. watch TV   3. go out to eat

Communicative drills, such as Exercise 4, did allow learners to answer truthfully rather than create an arbitrary answer to fit a structural pattern. Since the parties involved in the interaction did not already know the answers to the questions, the questions were considered open-ended. From these open-ended questions embedded in communicative drills, we experienced another evolution in communicatively oriented instructional practice. That is, instructors developed their use of open-ended questions based on paired drills and used questions to generate class discussions. Instructors intended to provide learners opportunities to express their own opinions and viewpoints without concurrently focusing on manipulating particular language structures. Imagine, then, the instructor who arrives to the classroom with a set of open-ended questions to ask the students, as in Exercise 5.

Exercise 5. Class Discussion

What did you (all) do last night?

Who studied?
[*Selecting a student.*]
>What did you study?
>Did you go to the library?

Who else went to the library?
[*Selecting a student.*]
>What did you study?
>Did you watch TV last night?
>What did you watch?

Did anyone go out to eat last night?
[*Selecting a student.*]
>Where did you go?
>What did you eat?
>With whom did you go?

The communication that results from the communicative drill and the class discussion can be characterized as a very simple dynamic: The authority-figure instructor asks the questions, the learners answer them. In Chapter 2 we will examine classroom practices and interactions that demonstrate a particular definition of communication: We shall see that for many instructors *communication = question & answer*. That is, when instructors communicate with their learners they do so by asking questions. Moreover, as the communicative practices just presented demonstrate, teaching materials support the notion that *communication = question & answer*. Lee and VanPatten (1995) critique the narrowness of this definition of communication as well as the primary, central, and unidimensional role the instructor plays in this classroom dynamic.

A different definition of communication is at the heart of this book. Communication is not equated with asking and answering questions; rather, communication is defined as the expression, interpretation, and negotiation of meaning. This definition is not new or unique to this book, but captures the thrust of authors such as Savignon (1997), Lee and VanPatten (1995), and Legutke and Thomas (1991). The concepts of expressing and interpreting meaning are not difficult to associate with communication since there must be a speaker and a listener in order for communication to take place. The relationship between negotiation and communication, however, may be less obvious. It is explained in the following part of the chapter.

WHY EMPHASIZE NEGOTIATION?

In this section, we will explore the following six reasons why both second language acquisition researchers and language teaching experts emphasize negotiation.

1. A theory of language acquisition
2. Classroom research
3. A social view of communication

4. Classroom practice
5. The optimal conditions for classroom second language acquisition
6. The insufficiency of input alone

We will discuss each in turn.

A Theory of Language Acquisition

Lightbown and Spada (1993) explain several theories of first and second language acquisition, among them the interactionist theory. The interactionists' position is that the linguistic environment (the language to which learners are exposed) is crucial to language development. In particular, language or input that is modified to suit the capabilities of the learner is a crucial element in the language acquisition process. Interactionists agree that comprehensible input is essential to language acquisition, but are most concerned with how the input is made comprehensible. Lightbown and Spada summarize the interactionist position as follows: "1. Interactional modification makes input comprehensible; 2. Comprehensible input promotes acquisition. Therefore, 3. Interactional modification promotes acquisition" (1993, p. 30). In short, the argument in favor of the relationship between acquisitional processes and interactional modifications (or negotiation of meaning) is a logical one (Crookes & Gass 1993a, 1993b; Long 1985).

Lightbown and Spada (1993) offer the following example of the type of interaction said to promote language acquisition. The example is of a 24-month-old child learning his first language. He is playing with a dump truck while two adults look on.

Interaction 1

1. PATSY: What happened to it (the truck)?
2. PETER: [*Looking under the chair for it.*] Lose it. Dump truck! Dump truck! Fall! Fall!
3. LOIS: Yes, the dump truck fell down.
4. PETER: Dump truck fell down. Dump truck.

Source: Lightbown & Spada 1993, p. 3.

Methods and approaches to language instruction may emphasize the selection of content, or *what* should be taught. Alternatively, they might emphasize *how* content should be taught. An important consideration that often is not fully accounted for is *why* something should be taught or *why* it should be taught in a particular way. Although different individuals may place different emphases on what, how, and why, the underlying principle of this book is that all three must constantly and explicitly be taken into consideration.

In line 3 the adult affirms the child's message and in doing so offers the child a grammatically correct rendering of the message he conveyed in line 2. In line 4, the child picks up and uses some of the language the adult just modeled.

The same type of interaction takes place in second language exchanges, too. The following example is part of a lesson presented in Chapter 4. Groups of adult classroom learners have worked together to prepare a list of ideas on how to become bicultural. They are presenting their ideas to the class. The interaction took place in Spanish in a third-semester, university-level Spanish class; it is translated into English for the benefit of the reader.

Interaction 2

85. GROUP 4: Visit other countries.

86. INSTRUCTOR: Visit and not live?

87. GROUP 4: No.

88. INSTRUCTOR: No? OK.

89. GROUP 4: Go to museum.

90. INSTRUCTOR: Ah. Go to a museum, to museums. In many big cities, in Chicago and also New York, there are museums, museums specifically dedicated to Hispanics, for example. And do you have other ideas?

91. GROUP 5: To tire of with another person who has another culture. [**Cansar** in Spanish = *to tire, become weary.*]

92. INSTRUCTOR: To tire of, no. To be tired is another thing. Get married? [**Casarse** in Spanish.] Marry someone from another culture or to have a girlfriend or boyfriend from another culture. That is a good way to begin to appreciate another culture.

In line 86 the instructor confirms that the group intended to say visit and not live in another country. In line 90 he accepts the group's idea that going to museums promotes biculturalism and then expands on the idea, offering the class more information. In line 91, the group uses a wrong word (**cansar** instead of **casarse**) and the instructor corrects it and then expands on the idea. Each time he expands on the learners' statements he is providing input as well as clarifying the learners' intended meanings.

The following exchange took place in a beginning ESL class at the secondary level. When the learners' linguistic expressions are not clear, the instructor maintains and supports the interaction by expanding on the learners' utterances. The result is that not only does the conversation keep moving forward, but the learners receive a grammatically correct representation of what they intended to express.

Interaction 3

1. INSTRUCTOR: Vin, have you ever been to the movies? What's your favorite movie?

2. VIN: *Big.*

3. INSTRUCTOR: *Big*, OK, that's a good movie, that was about a little boy inside a big man, wasn't it?

4. VIN: Yeah, boy get surprise all the time.

5. INSTRUCTOR: Yes, he was surprised, wasn't he? Usually little boys don't do the things that men do, do they?

6. VIN: No, little boy no drink.

7. INSTRUCTOR: That's right, little boys don't drink.

8. WANG: *Kung Fu.*

9. INSTRUCTOR: *Kung Fu?* You like the movie *Kung Fu?*

10. WANG: Yeah . . . fight.

11. INSTRUCTOR: That was about a great fighter? . . . A man who knows how to fight with his hands.

12. WANG: I fight . . . my hand.

13. INSTRUCTOR: You know how to fight with your hands?
14. WANG: I fight with my hand.
15. INSTRUCTOR: Do you know karate?
16. WANG: I know karate.
17. INSTRUCTOR: Watch out, guys, Wang knows karate.
Source: Adapted from Johnson 1995, pp. 23–24.

Although research has yet to determine exactly what role these expansions play in language acquisition, it is clear that the learners receive an accurate linguistic model of what they intended to say.

The relationship between interaction and acquisition has been established logically, but empirical evidence has emerged that also favors the interactionist theory of language acquisition. Mackey (1995) examined two experimental groups of learners and a control group. (Her research is more detailed and complex than can be described here, so we will highlight only certain aspects of the work.) One group participated in interaction and another observed the interaction. In a sense, Mackey established an output group and an input group of beginning and lower-intermediate ESL learners. The experimental procedures lasted a week, during which non-native speakers completed task-based activities with native speakers. In all, they did twelve activities. The observers observed twelve activities. The subjects were all non-native speakers of English, and the targeted linguistic item was question formation. The research question was how many subjects would move to the next stage of acquisition. In the control group, only one of seven "naturally" moved to the next stage of acquisition. Five of the seven who interacted, that is, produced language, moved to the next stage. And four of the seven who observed interaction moved to the next stage. The latter finding attests to the power and importance of input. Over time, however, Mackey found some differences. One week and one month later, the interaction group continued its linguistic development, but the observers remained static. They held onto their initial increase but did not improve further.

Mackey's findings are fascinating. They support Krashen's Input Hypothesis (Krashen & Terrell 1983) as well as the Output Hypothesis (Swain 1985). They certainly affirm the emphasis that second language researchers place on negotiation and the emphasis second language teachers place on tasks.

Classroom Research

Research has investigated classroom activities that promote the type of interaction that leads to speech modifications. Typically, two activities are compared. One activity is led by the instructor (i.e., teacher-fronted) such that the learners interact primarily if not exclusively with the instructor but only rarely if ever with each other. The other activity involves paired or group learner-to-learner interaction. The instructor's involvement in the interaction is minimized. The underlying assumption in this research is that, since interactional modifications are important for language acquisition, what circumstances bring about the greatest number of such modifications? Several empirical investigations have compared teacher-fronted activities with paired/group work that required negotiation (Doughty & Pica 1986; Porter 1986; Rulon & McCreary 1986). The findings of this line of research have been quite consistent. Not only did individual learners have more opportunities to use the language, they also had more opportunities to use the language communicatively. That is, when paired/group work entails negotiation, the paired/group interactions yield more content clarifications (efforts to clarify what has not been understood), confirmation checks (indications that what has been understood has been understood correctly), and comprehension checks (efforts to determine that a listener has understood a message). These interactional modifications are the linguistic evidence that negotiation takes place and, as such, the input is being made comprehensible to those involved in the interaction (Lightbown & Spada 1993; Long 1983).

A Social View of Communication

The concept of negotiation in second language acquisition has been tightly linked to the idea of breakdowns in communication and miscomprehensions, as the following citations attest. Brooks states that "negotiation of meaning is said to take place when communication problems that arise during a conversation are resolved" (1992, p. 64). Some refer to negotiations as "interruptions" in that the flow of conversation is stopped; topic development ceases in order to resolve the difficulty in understanding (Gass & Selinker 1994). The Varonis and Gass model of negotiation concurs, labeling elements of the communication *indications, triggers,* and *responses.* They refer to negotiative language use as a *discourse subroutine* that happens in order to regain the place in the conversation when one or both interlocutors have slipped (1985, p. 73). Negotiation, from this perspective, happens as an aside and is a process engaged in to compensate for incomplete comprehension.

Perhaps the most complete definition of negotiation from this perspective is found in Pica (1992), who states that "the label negotiation has been applied to those interactions in which learners and their interlocutors adjust their speech phonologically, lexically, and morphosyntactically to resolve difficulties in mutual understanding that impede the course of their communication" (p. 200). In Pica's analyses, "negotiation was defined as an activity that occurs when a listener signals to a speaker that the speaker's message is not clear, and listener and speaker modify their speech to resolve this impasse" (p. 200).

Although a proponent of negotiation in classroom interaction, Kinginger (1996) takes exception to justifying classroom practice around negotiative language use as presented in the previous section. She states, "This line of research is fundamentally limited by an asocial view of communication. In the mass of this research, the findings are quantifications of problems learners encounter, with recommendations as to productiveness of particular [materials] formats based solely on the number of documented instances of trouble. Is it really so wise—from a pedagogical viewpoint—to recommend particular task types as 'empirically demonstrated acquisition settings' based solely on how many times they frustrate learners' attempts to make sense?" (p. 1) She and others working in a Vygotskyan framework would deemphasize a justification based on analyzing linguistic elements of speech in favor of an argument that attends to the interpersonal, dynamic, and context-specific nature of communication (Brooks & Donato 1994). Vygotsky (1978) focuses on social processes that contribute to cognitive development. He argues that learning and cognitive development are interrelated; cognition develops as a result of social interaction. As Brooks, Donato, and McGlone (1997, p. 525) explain, speaking, thinking, and acting should not be seen as three separate activities, but as activities that constitute each other. They give the example of a recipe. The individual ingredients can be viewed separately and individually on a kitchen counter, but the appropriate way to view them is how they coalesce to become something greater than themselves. Proponents of a social view of communication maintain that an individual's language development is a by-product of socially mediated forms of interaction (p. 534).

Kinginger (1996) points out that a pedagogically logical definition of negotiation cannot be based solely in discourse subroutines aimed at resolving impasses in communication, that is, instances when speakers leave the main topic of discussion, resolve their miscomprehensions, and then return to the topic of discussion. Negotiative language use must be the principal discourse routine rather than an interruption and need not, therefore, be linked to miscomprehensions or other impediments to understanding. In other words, negotiative language use must be the point of the interaction and not something that happens only when speakers misunderstand each other.

Taking a social view of communication along with classroom research and an interactionist perspective on language acquisition, we can propose a pedagogically logical definition of negotiation. The following definition underlies the approach to task-based instruction presented in this book.

> *Negotiation* consists of interactions during which speakers come to terms, reach an agreement, make arrangements, resolve a problem, or settle an issue by conferring or discussing; the purpose of language use is to accomplish some task rather than to practice any particular language forms.

Classroom Practices

This chapter began by demonstrating a connection between audiolingual, form-oriented practices and certain communicative practices. Communicative practices in which learners ask and answer questions do not fulfill the definition of communication that guides this work. Research has shown that students who are given communicative drills to perform in pairs, such as Exercises 2 and 4 presented earlier in the chapter, tend to focus on the drill aspects of the practice and not on the communication (Brooks 1990; Kinginger 1990). That is, if learners discern that the manipulation of forms is at the heart of an exercise, they focus on such manipulation. Even though instructors believe they are fulfilling the charge of providing their learners opportunities to communicate, the learners are not communicating with each other as much as they are drilling each other. As Brooks documents, one of the learners in the pair often reenacts the instructor's role, even to the point of offering words of encouragement or, as in the following exchange, corrective feedback to the partner.

Interaction 4

1. s1: Por favor, señor, ¿cómo son Luisa?
2. s2: ¿Cómo son o cómo es?

3. s1: Would that be *cómo es?* Wouldn't it be? *¿Cómo es Luisa?*
4. s2: *Luisa es muy simpática.*
5. s1: *Muy simpática.*
Source: Adapted from Brooks 1990, p. 159.

Translation

1. s1: Please, sir, how are Luisa?
2. s2: How are or how is?
3. s1: Would that be how is? Wouldn't it be? How is Luisa?
4. s2: Luisa is very nice.
5. s1: Very nice.

Although there is some expression, interpretation, and negotiation taking place, the learners are not expressing, interpreting, and negotiating meaning, but form. The materials do not support the instructor's intent to provide the learners opportunities to communicate.

Optimal Conditions for Classroom Second Language Acquisition

Ellis (1990) reviews several theories of second language acquisition from which he extrapolates the optimal conditions for classroom second language acquisition. Van Lier (1991) also proposes some optimal conditions on language learning that emphasize the importance of having learners progress from noticing the language they are exposed to, to understanding it, and then to using it appropriately. A combined set of optimal conditions are the following.

1. Learners must be receptive to the language they are exposed to.
2. Learners must have an investment in learning, a need and desire to process the language.
3. Learners must have a need and desire to communicate.
4. Learners require abundant opportunities to control the topic of conversation and to self-initiate in the classroom.
5. Instructors and learners must make the effort to be understood (which involves negotiating meaning).
6. Learners must be challenged to operate beyond their current level of competence.
7. Learners need abundant opportunities to perform a range of illocutionary or communicative functions with the second language.
8. Instructors must provide opportunities for learners to participate in planned and unplanned discourse similar to what they will encounter outside the classroom.
9. Instructors should provide sufficient models of discourse containing many samples of the linguistic features that learners are trying to learn.
10. Learner output should not be forced; learners should be free to self-select when they participate.

These optimal conditions for classroom second language emphasize the negotiation of meaning as the means by which to structure discourse.

The Insufficiency of Input Alone

Lee and VanPatten (1995) distinguish the roles input and output play in second language development. *Input* is the language learners are exposed to and contains the linguistic data they need to construct their second-language grammatical systems. Clearly, constructing a second-language system depends upon the input available to the learner. *Output* is the language learners themselves produce. The role output plays in language development is to push learners to develop communicative language ability—the ability to express oneself and to understand others. Learners do not develop communicative language ability without producing the language. Swain (1985) argues that producing comprehensible output helps learners become better processors of comprehensible input. In order to produce output, learners must access their linguistic systems and access does not follow automatically from acquiring a form (Terrell 1986, 1991). In short, while input processing is linked to acquiring form and structure, access is linked to accuracy or correctness and fluency or ease and speed of production. Language learners, then, must have opportunities to create language. The emphasis on negotiation follows from the concept of communicative language ability and how best to create the opportunities for learners to create language.

SUMMARY

The purpose of this chapter was to introduce and discuss two crucial concepts, communication and negotiation. We began with a brief account of Audiolingual Methodology to demonstrate a connection between a grammar or form-oriented approach to instruction and communicative approaches to language teaching. The point made was that communicative language teaching practices evolved from grammar-oriented ones. As language teachers began to acknowledge that part of their charge was to provide learners opportunities to use the language, they relied on practices and activities that embody questions and answers. In fact, communication was equated with instructors asking questions and learners answering them. This notion that *communication = question & answer* has been rejected in this book. Instead, the definition that motivates this book is that communication is the expression, interpretation, and negotiation of meaning.

An emphasis on negotiation was explained referring to six concepts: a theory of language acquisition, classroom research on teacher-fronted versus paired/group work, a social view of communication, classroom practices, the optimal conditions for classroom second language acquisition, and the insufficiency of input alone in developing communicative language ability. The interactionist theory of language acquisition, be it first or second language acquisition, recognizes the importance of comprehensible input in language development but views interactional modifications as crucial to making input comprehensible. Classroom research has consistently demonstrated that more interactional modifications or negotiation of meaning takes place in paired/group activities than in teacher-fronted activities. A social view of communication demands that negotiation of meaning not only be connected to breakdowns in communication as those engaged in the classroom research have examined it, but that negotiation be the fabric of instructional practice. We will explore this concept in Chapter 3. But taking these issues together, we proposed a pedagogically logical definition of negotiation as interactions during which speakers come to terms, reach an agreement, make arrangements, resolve a problem, or settle an issue by conferring or discussing; the purpose of language use is to accomplish some task rather than to practice any particular language forms. We then examined classroom practices that lead learners to focus on manipulating forms rather than communicating ideas. Based on reviews of research, optimal conditions for acquiring a second language in a classroom (as opposed to a natural setting) lead to an emphasis on negotiation. Structuring communication so that negotiation of meaning takes place is one of the optimal conditions. Finally, researchers agree that the role of input in second language acquisition is to provide the linguistic data necessary for developing the second-language linguistic system. The role of output is to develop accuracy and fluency in the second language. Output is necessary for developing communicative language ability, which involves not only expressing oneself but interpreting the messages that come back.

In Chapter 2, we will more fully explore how communication takes place in classrooms by examining six excerpts from language classes. We will examine the types of decisions instructors make about communication while they interact with learners.

GAINING GREATER PERSPECTIVE

1. *Language Development.* Lightbown and Spada (1993) present several theories of first and second language acquisition. Their work is extremely comprehensible to those who are not familiar with a wider body of literature.
2. *Audiolingual Methodology.* Richards and Rogers (1986) describe and analyze Audiolingual Methodology. They provide both historical background and examples of teaching materials. Lightbown and Spada (1993) provide a sample of instructor-learner interaction in an audiolingual class (Chapter 5).
3. *From ALM to Communicative Language Teaching.* To get the sense of evolution rather than revolution, read Chapters 1 and 2 of Savignon (1983). An influential methodologist, Wilga Rivers, wrote several works on language teaching that today are clearly situated in this interim, evolving period. See, for example, Rivers (1972). During this interim period, Paulston (1978) recommended that instructors sequence their drills from mechanical to meaningful to communicative. This work is worth reading in and of itself and is discussed in Lee and VanPatten (1995) as it relates to current thinking on grammar instruction.
4. *Negotiation.* Pica (1992) is an excellent summary of a large body of research on negotiation from the perspective of communication breakdowns.

APPLICATION ACTIVITIES

1. Prove something to yourself about the meaningfulness of substitution drills. Read over the following substitution drill for object pronouns in Spanish (which must agree in number and gender with the noun they refer to), and carry out the indicated substitutions.

   Juan pone los vasos en la mesa. → Juan **los** pone en la mesa.
   (las copas, la comida, el plato, la cafetera, las tortillas)
   John puts the glasses on the table. → John puts them on the table.

   Now, carry out the drill with the following nonsense words.

   Juan gaga los momos en la posa. → Juan **los** gaga en la posa.
   (las ponas, la loga, el blapo, la terefaca, las sillortas)

   Could you carry out the substitutions successfully? If learners can carry out an activity without understanding anything they are saying, what are they learning about the language?

2. Sit in a cafeteria, lounge, or café and eavesdrop on conversations taking place around you. Note examples of how people negotiate meaning. Can you find examples of negotiation that occurs due to miscomprehensions (as in Pica's work)? Can you find examples of negotiation that exemplifies the union of speaking, thinking, and acting (as in Kinginger's and Brooks, Donato, & McGlone's work)?

3. The following transcript contains part of the interaction between three female students enrolled in first-semester Spanish. They are taking an oral test (described in detail in Chapter 9). The activity is about interesting people. In the first part (lines 21–37), they are discussing the most interesting person in the class. At line 38, they begin discussing the most interesting person in the United States. s1 and s3 have the same male instructor; s2 has a female instructor. Read over the interaction and determine whether a social view of communication or communication breakdowns best characterize the way in which the learners interact.

   21. s2: [*Reads from activity sheet.*] Who is interesting in Spanish class?
   22. s3: Your professor.
   23. s1: Yes, my professor in my Spanish.
   24. s3: We are professor is short.
   25. s1: My professor is short. His hair is curly? But very, very interesting.
   26. s3: Yes, he is, he is not boring.
   27. s2: My professor is very, very cute and tall.
   28. s3: And shoes is tall, *also.*
   29. s1: My professor is very nice, is, um, he is very, um, interesting but ah . . .
   30. s3: The professor has dark hair and straight.
   31. s2: And dark eyes.
   32. s3: Blue.
   33. s2: Blue, yes.

34. s3: Yes.

35. s1: My professor explains directions very well, he, the class.

36. s2: But my professor doesn't . . .

37. s3: Doesn't speak English. [*Laughter.*]

38. s2: OK, Step 3, please. Um, the president is the most interesting in the United States.

39. s3: Yes, he is intelligent.

40. s1: He is boring, boring.

41. s3: He is ugly. He is ugly.

42. s2: But you have a talent for leadership. [*Laughter.*]

43. s1: The president speaks very, very . . .

44. s2: Boring.

45. s1: Boring.

46. s3: He is ugly.

47. s1: But he is logical, [*uninterpretable word*] on television.

48. s2: Do you think ugly or cute?

49. s1: Ugly.

50. s3: Ugly, a lot ugly. He is, um . . .

51. s2: Big nose.

52. s3: Yes, um, red hair.

53. s1: He plays football in um . . .

54. s3: College.

CHAPTER 2

Communicating in the Language Classroom

CHAPTER OVERVIEW

As defined in Chapter 1, *communication* is the expression, interpretation, and negotiation of meaning. In order for language learners to engage in communication, they must be given opportunities to say what they mean and to work toward a mutual understanding with other interlocutors (be they instructors or other learners). The purpose of this chapter is to examine interactions between instructors and learners that take place in "communicatively oriented" classrooms, in order to demonstrate a particular type of classroom communication and how the expression, interpretation, and negotiation of meaning does not happen in classrooms. The three different instructors whose classes are analyzed intended to create communicative lessons; they intended to provide learners opportunities for language use. Note that all instructors volunteered to have their classes recorded for research purposes.

THE NATURE OF CLASSROOM DISCOURSE

Classroom language is a much studied domain of communication research and has been described as a game with explicit as well as implicit rules (Belleck, Kliebard, Hyman, & Smith 1966). These are specialized rules and expectations for appropriate instructor and learner communicative behaviors (Cazden 1986). Classroom discourse has been characterized as adhering to, or being a slight variation on, a sequence of verbal acts: a teacher-initiated act (I), a learner-response act (R), and a teacher-evaluation act (E), often referred to by the acronym IRE (Mehan 1979; Sinclair & Coulthard 1975). Brooks (1992) has referred to this pattern in language classrooms as a ping-pong game of questions and answers. As Johnson indicates, "the teacher sets up the rules of the game, is the most active player, and acts as the solicitor while students act as respondents. . . . The IRE pattern allows teachers to maintain control over the structure of classroom communication; at the same time, however, students must be able to recognize that structure and learn to speak within it" (1995, pp. 9–10). In the following three lessons, we find this pattern of classroom discourse. We will signal certain important problems in adhering to IRE as the sole sequence of verbal acts between instructors and learners.

LESSON 1

Lesson 1 took place in a first-year Spanish language class the day before the midterm exam was administered. This introductory course covers the content of 1 year of university-level Spanish in 1 semester and is designed for students with 2 or more years of high school Spanish but who want or need to start their Spanish language instruction from the beginning. The instructor who taught Lesson 1 was not a native speaker of Spanish and had limited teaching experience, consisting of 1 semester prior to the one examined. During that semester, the instructor had taken a course on communicative language teaching. All sections of the course share a common syllabus; students take common exams and are evaluated using common criteria. In this sense, then, the department—not the individual instructor—controls materials and the curriculum. Even so, the class day examined in this research can be characterized as a "free" day, one without departmentally driven expectations of what should happen in class or how it should happen. On this day, the instructor had the freedom to choose materials and structure the class session. The instructor created the materials independent of external constraints. In analyzing the class session, we can truly examine how this particular instructor created events she thought were communicative. The class was conducted entirely into Spanish (the excerpts have been translated into English for the convenience of the reader).

Lesson 1 can be divided into four segments, presented in Figure 2.1. This lesson plan is communicatively oriented: An observer can plainly see the attempt to provide learners a lesson in which they use the target language. The central activity of creating a person required collaborative group work and provided a long, extended period of learner-to-learner interaction (25 minutes). The task of cutting out and putting together a unique person was meant to provide the learners a little fun before taking the midterm exam the next day. This activity was preceded by a segment that reviewed material pertinent to the activity and was followed by having the class present and compare their creations.

Excerpt 1   Assuming Responsibility

The instructor gave the class 25 minutes to create their persons. Each group then wrote a description of its person and read it to the class. The instructor directed the class to listen to the descriptions in order to compare and contrast them. Excerpt 1 contains one group's reading of its description and the instructor's response. Read Excerpt 1 and, as you do, consider the function and impact of the instructor's series of questions in lines 6–14. Note that the instructor responded the same way to all five groups.

> I. Instructor distributes a handout of the direction lines and sample questions from the upcoming exam.
> II. Instructor restates the content of the previous day's lesson, then reviews one aspect of the lesson, i.e., colors, because it is used in III (below).
> III. Instructor divides the class into groups of four to carry out the following activity.
>> **Step 1.** The group cuts out body parts from a sheet provided and pastes them together to create an "original" person.
>> **Step 2.** The group writes a description of its person and reads it to the class.
>> **Step 3.** After groups read their descriptions, the class compares them (looking for similarities among the descriptions).
> IV. Instructor initiates an impromptu discussion of the advantages and disadvantages of having a twin. Time runs out during this discussion.

FIGURE 2.1 Segments of Lesson 1

Excerpt 1. Assuming Responsibility

1. ɪ: Aahh, the group with [*inaudible*] is going to present.
2. s: He is Juan.
3. s: [*Laughter.*]
4. ɪ: He is Juan. OK.
5. s: [*Inaudible*] and very different. Juan has four, four eyes, yellow and two mouths. Two orange mouths. Juan has . . . a green [*inaudible*]. Juan has . . . a black hair. Juan's nose is strange. Juan is very fat. And he has one arm and he has one arm and one hand. A hand and Juan has three pink legs.
6. ɪ: Very good. What is his name?
7. s: Juan.
8. ɪ: And what color is his face?
9. s: Green.
10. ɪ: And his hand, what color?
11. s: Blue.
12. ɪ: What is ahh, what on Juan is pink? What is pink?
13. s: His legs.
14. ɪ: His legs. And how many legs does he have?
15. s: Three.
16. ɪ: Three. Very good. OK. The group with . . . Erin is going to present to us now. Can everyone see Erin's group?

Before the first group presented its description, the instructor told the class to pay attention to the other groups' descriptions, to think about what they would hear, and that they would discuss the descriptions. From a communicative perspective, the instructor created conditions conducive to the expression, interpretation, and negotiation of meaning in that the class members had a reason and purpose to listen to each other. In essence, class members were to gather the information they would need to discuss the descriptions.

But as Excerpt 1 shows, the instructor's verbal behavior removed the need for learners to negotiate meaning with each other when she asked a series of questions. The instructor repeated this pattern of asking questions after each of the five groups had read its description. What purpose did these questions serve? Surely these questions were not comprehension checks. Surely the instructor did not need these questions to confirm what she understood. How could she not have understood all five descriptions? Surely these questions were not clarification requests; they were much too precisely worded and, more revealingly, were asked five times to the five different groups.

Teaching can be described and accounted for as a series of decisions. Instructors make decisions prior to entering a classroom: materials selection, materials sequencing, timing, etc. Instructors also then make decisions as they act on their previous decisions. Teaching happens "in the moment" and, as such, an instructor makes decisions "in the moment." As we see in Excerpt 1, the instructor made good decisions about the materials prior to coming to class, but then made questionable decisions "in the moment." The quality of the decisions differs significantly.

Whereas the learners were supposed to be providing information and reporting to each other, each group, in fact, reported to the instructor. The instructor did not allow the learners to be responsible for their own comprehension. No learner ever questioned another group, even though the learners were the ones who needed the information and who were supposed to use the information. In a real sense, the learners ended up being bystanders at what was intended to be a communicative event.

Excerpt 2   An Impromptu Discussion

After groups presented their descriptions and the instructor asked them questions, the class made comparisons across the descriptions. In the course of having learners make comparative statements, the instructor suggested that two of the created people might be twins (the names given to these people are Wido and Pepe). To bring closure to the lesson, she tried to engage the class in an impromptu discussion of whether having a twin is an advantage. As you read over Excerpt 2, examine who asked the questions. Did learners ask questions or did they only answer them?

Excerpt 2. Impromptu Discussion
1.   I: So, if they [*Wido and Pepe*] are twins, we're going to explore, is it, is it good or bad to have twins? Do you understand me? To be twins. Do you understand me?
2. ss[1]: Yes.
3.   I: Now we are going to see if it is good to have a twin or if it's bad to have a twin. OK?
4. ss: [*No answer.*]
5.   I: Another word that we can use, more sophisticated, do you understand sophisticated?

---

[1]ss refers to two or more students answering, s to a single student.

6. ss: Yes.

7. I: We can say advantage or disadvantage. Yes? Does everyone understand?

8. ss: [*No answer.*]

9. I: Does everyone understand?

10. ss: Yes.

11. I: Let's see. Who can think of an advantage, of an advantage of being a twin?

12. s: [*Inaudible.*]

13. I: OK. Pepe. OK. Ah! OK. Only that Pepe is the advantage and Wido the disadvantage.

14. ss: [*Laughter.*]

15. I: Good. What do twins do?

16. ss: [*No answer.*]

17. I: Is anyone here a twin? Does anyone know some twins? Yes, Kimberly and David. Is it good or bad to have a twin?

18. s: Both.

19. I: Both. It's good. Why? Why is it good?

20. s: Ahh. They can talk with other people.

21. I: Ah. OK. They have a person with whom to talk. They have a friend. So, an advantage is that friends . . . you have a friend. [*Bell rings.*] Oh, it's time already. Good. We'll continue a little tomorrow, after the test. Goodbye, and don't forget to leave your doll on the desk.

The instructor relied on the question and answer format to engage the class in a discussion: She asked the questions, the learners answered them. The number of learners answering questions, in this excerpt, was only two. Although the discussion reached no conclusion due to time constraints, it suffered from what most whole-class discussions tend to suffer from. First, since the discussion involved only a few people and excluded many more than it included, it does not fulfill the definition of discussion as "the consideration of a subject by a group" (*American Heritage Dictionary* 1973, p. 377). Second, the exchanges were linguistically lopsided extractions rather than considerations of a topic. That is, the instructor's questions served to extract the subject from the learners rather than have instructor and learners exchange ideas.

LESSON 2

Lesson 2 took place in the same first-year Spanish course as Lesson 1, but took place 2 days later, the day after the midterm exam was administered. The instructor who taught Lesson 2 was a native speaker of Spanish. She had limited teaching experience, consisting of 1 semester prior to the one examined. During that semester, the instructor had taken a course on communicative language teaching. The class session analyzed was conducted entirely in Spanish (the excerpts have been translated into English for the convenience of the reader). Even though each section of the course shares a common syllabus, and students take common exams and are evaluated using common criteria, the day after the midterm exam can be characterized as a "free" day, one without departmentally driven expectations of what should happen in class or

I. Talk about the exam last night
II. Music video: preparation
   A. class divided first into groups of three and then into groups of five
   B. class answers questions in order to build background knowledge
      1. types of relationships
      2. types of emotions
      3. famous couples
   C. instructor assigns class to read print version of song, and in groups they answer written comprehension questions about printed lyrics
   D. instructor does over some items.
III. Music video: viewing
   A. class watches music video
   B. groups sing stanzas of the song (twice)
   C. instructor chooses the group that sang the best
   D. instructor finishes going over questions about print version (II C)
   E. instructor assigns groups to answer comprehension questions about music video
   F. instructor goes over some items
IV. Discussion of how people change (a theme of the song)
V. Leavetaking

FIGURE 2.2 Segments of Lesson 2

how it should happen. On this day, the instructor chose the materials and structured the class session. Just as with Lesson 1, we can examine how a particular instructor created events she thought were communicative.

Lesson 2 can be divided into the five segments presented in Figure 2.2. Since this lesson took place the day after the midterm exam, its goals were limited to something close to just getting through the 50 minutes. Even so, the lesson plan is meant to be communicatively oriented: An observer can plainly see the attempt to provide learners a lesson in which they comprehend language (presented musically) in order to discuss a theme. The two central activities involve reading the lyrics of a song and watching the music video. Several other, satellite activities take place, such as building background knowledge and a singing contest. Whereas 25 minutes of Lesson 1 were spent in group work, only 12 of Lesson 2 were. Both group assignments in Lesson 2 required learners to answer comprehension questions, one set about the lyrics and the other about the music video. The learners spent perhaps 3 minutes watching the video and the remaining 35 minutes listening to the instructor.

Excerpt 3   Communication = Question & Answer

In Excerpt 2 from Lesson 1, the instructor attempted to conduct a class discussion using a question and answer format. In Excerpt 3, the instructor also wanted to conduct a discussion and also relied on asking questions to do so. As you read Excerpt 3, pay attention to the learners' responses. A dictionary definition of conversation is an "informal exchange of thoughts and feelings" (*American Heritage Dictionary* 1973, p. 291). Did the learners have a conversation with the instructor?

Excerpt 3. Communication = Question & Answer

1. I: Love, also, OK. So. Love is, it is a very popular and common emotion. No? Yes?
2. SS: Yes.
3. I: Is it better to love or to hate?
4. SS: [*No answer.*]
5. I: Or to detest?
6. SS: [*No answer.*]
7. I: What?
8. SS: [*No answer.*]
9. I: Or maybe. It's. Let's. Ah. Is it better, emotion, to love or is it a better emotion to hate? to detest?
10. SS: Love.
11. SS: Love.
12. I: Love. OK. Why is it a better relationship?
13. SS: [*No answer.*]
14. I: Or emotion?
15. SS: [*No answer.*]
16. I: Love or hate?
17. SS: [*No answer.*]
18. I: Any ideas?
19. S: It, it's more fun.
20. I: OK. Very good. It's more fun. Yes.
21. SS: [*Laughter.*]

The instructor wanted learners to compare two emotions, love and hate, and asked a series of questions to elicit their responses. The resulting silences were, however, deafening. Since there were no respondents, we can ask, Who was the instructor having this conversation with? One immediate answer is that she was conversing with herself. One-sidedness is all too often the result of teacher-fronted question-and-answer sessions when communication relies on one person asking all the questions. How often have we, as instructors, felt that we are talking to ourselves when standing in front of a classroom? Without respondents there can be no communication.

Excerpt 4 Gratuitous Group Work

Gratuitous means unnecessary, unwarranted, or unjustified. To define group work as gratuitous, we must examine the task itself, how the task is assigned, how the group carries out the task, and whether the products of the group work are woven into the remainder of the lesson. Just what group work is gratuitous will be situation-specific, but we can watch for the following. First, gratuitous group work entails learner-to-learner interactions that do not require learners to negotiate meaning. Does the task require interaction as a requisite to being completed? Second, gratuitous group work entails products of group interaction for which the learners or groups are not subsequently responsible in the lesson. What is the purpose of the group work? Would the same purpose be achieved via non-group interaction?

This second lesson, in contrast to the first, required no more than 12 minutes of group work. Both times the instructor assigned learners to group interaction, the task was the same: They had to answer comprehension questions. Read Excerpt 4 and, as you do, consider whether the learners needed to work with each other to answer the questions.

Excerpt 4.   Gratuitous Group Work

1.   ɪ: Yes? So. Take like, a minute or two, one, one minute or two, to read the song before we see the video. Is that OK?
2.   ss: Yes.
3.   ɪ: Go. Read. OK?

[*Students work for 2 minutes.*]

4.   ɪ: When you finish, do number . . . three, which is on the other side of the page. The questions, unfortunately, are in English. OK? You are going to read them in English, but you are going to speak in Spanish.
5.   s: Spanish.
6.   ɪ: Right? That way you do number three in groups. OK. And I am going to give you some 4 minutes to do this. Is that OK?
7.   ss: [*No answer.*]

[*Students work in groups for 5 minutes as instructor walks among them.*]

8.   ɪ: Good. I believe that our time is up. What group has 3a?
9.   ss: [*No answer.*]
10.   ɪ: Group that wants to answer 3a?
11.   ss: [*No answer.*]
12.   ɪ: Any volunteer? Dan's group, here.
13.   s: [*Inaudible.*]
14.   ɪ: OK. An a-abandoned relationship. OK. Any other answer?
15.   ss: [*No answer.*]
16.   ɪ: Something different?
17.   ss: [*No answer.*]
18.   ɪ: Does anyone have something different?
19.   ss: [*No answer.*]
20.   ɪ: Amy?
21.   s: [*Inaudible.*]
22.   ɪ: OK. Did everybody hear?
23.   ss: [*No answer.*]
24.   ɪ: The couples do not have trust. OK. What else? Does this song—this relationship talk about friendship?
25.   ss: [*No answer.*]
26.   ɪ: Does it talk about friendship? Yes?
27.   ss: Y-y-yes.
28.   ɪ: Yes. I believe that it does.

Learners could have worked individually just as well as cooperatively to answer a series of comprehension questions. The task did not require learner-to-learner interaction. Whether learners had worked together to answer the questions or individually would not have affected the outcome of the activity. The product of their interaction—that is, the correct answers to the questions—did not depend on the learners interacting.

Linguistically, the instructor's follow-up, which begins in line 8, was no different from that in any other part of the lesson: It was firmly rooted in the *communication = question & answer* paradigm. More important, simply asking someone from the group for the answer did not require the group to be responsible for deriving the answer or the rest of the class to be responsible for attending to the answer. The instructor would have needed to know how many in the class got the right answer and/or have had the group explain its selection to those who did not get the right answer. The instructor did not connect any group's response to how the rest of the class responded. The result was that the answers were just loose pieces of unconnected information left hanging in the air. Contrast the gratuitousness of this group work with the purposefulness of the group work in Lesson 1, for which the groups wrote descriptions, presented them, and then made comparisons across descriptions.

Excerpt 5   Communication Curtailed

While going over the answers to the comprehension questions, the instructor orchestrated a singing contest for which she acted as the judge and jury. In Excerpt 5, the instructor ended the contest by selecting the best vocal performance (lines 1–9). At this point, she began to discuss with the class the reasons for their vocal performances. As you read Excerpt 5, pay attention to lines 9–19. Instructor and learners exchange information, but what happens in lines 15–18?

Excerpt 5.   Communication Curtailed

1. I: I believe that you sang better. I'm sorry. It's sad. Very good. What group won? Or was everyone horrible?
2. SS: [*No answer.*]
3. I: Did any group win?
4. S: Oh, us.
5. I: Erin says that they won. Is that true?
6. SS: [*No answer.*]
7. I: Kurt's group. There, zero points.
8. SS: [*Laughter.*]
9. I: OK? Zero points. Nadine's group began more or less well, but it finished baaaadly. They sank to the bottom and here, Brian, I don't know what happened. Brian, what happened?
10. S: Fast.
11. I: It is very fast.
12. S: Oh. It's easy.
13. S: Oh, it's not fair.
14. I: Well, at best, it's possible that Erin's group won.
15. S: It's easy.
16. I: OK. It's easy. For that reason?
17. S: Noo.

18. I: OK. Excuses, excuses. Do you understand excuses? Cognate.

19. SS: Yes.

Excerpt 5 stands out in the transcript of the 50-minute class period as the only time the instructor did not engage the *communication = question & answer* paradigm. Rather, she made statements and comments about the singing. When the instructor asks in line 9, "What happened?" she began a genuine communicative exchange with some learners. They expressed themselves. The instructor interpreted their statements. The learners and instructor then mutually negotiated an understanding. Three learners offered reasons for their vocal performances (lines 10 and 12) and commented that her judgments were unfair (line 13). She seemed to ignore the comment in that she did not address fairness in her response in line 14. One learner said the word *easy* in lines 12 and 15. It is unclear whether the reference was to the learners' vocal performance or to the instructor's judgment but the instructor did acknowledge the comment in line 16 by repeating the learner's statement and questioning him. The learner responded negatively in line 17 to the instructor's question; the negative response apparently disconfirmed the previous understanding toward which the learner and instructor had been working. The response should have triggered more negotiation because understanding had not been achieved. In line 18, the instructor exercised her authority over the interaction and terminated it by humorously calling the learners' comments excuses. The communication was curtailed.

> **The instructional goals of covering material and moving a lesson forward to completion sometimes conflict with the instructional goals of providing learners opportunities to participate in the lesson and use the target language. It takes time for learners to participate and it takes time for learners to use the target language. "Learner time," then, is a critical factor to consider as instructors make their decisions prior to entering the classroom.**

LESSON 3

Leeman Guthrie was among the earliest to question the use of questions as the basis of classroom communicative exchanges. She recorded a series of class sessions, including Excerpt 6 that follows. Lesson 3 took place in a second-semester introductory French class. Leeman Guthrie does not provide specific information on the instructor who conducted Lesson 3, but states that the various instructors she examined were graduate students in their second semester of teaching. In other words, their profiles would be similar to those instructors who taught Lessons 1 and 2.

Excerpt 6   Poor Claudia

The discussion in Excerpt 6 is a follow-up to a reading on stereotypes presented in the learners' textbook. The original exchange took place in French, except for the student's request in line 6. Can you determine what Claudia's opinion is?

Excerpt 6.   Poor Claudia

1. ɪ: So you think there is really one French personality, a typically French personality? Yes?

2. ss: No.

3. ɪ: No? Why? [*Pause.*] Claudia?

4. s: Um . . . I think that there's a—

5. ɪ: [*Interrupting.*] That there's a French personality? Good. Describe the French personality.

6. s: *How do you say "pride"?*

7. ɪ: Oh . . . You've already had two words. [*Writing on blackboard.*] Okay, "la fierté" is like in English *"pride,"* and the adjective, "fier." Je suis fier, *I'm proud.* Good, are the French very proud? Do they have a lot of pride? [*Silence.*] Are the French nationalistic?

Source: Adapted from Leeman Guthrie 1984, p. 53.

The similarities between Excerpt 6, the impromptu discussion of twins in Excerpt 2, and the discussion of emotions in Excerpt 3 are striking. Whereas the goal of this language instructor was to provide the learners opportunities to communicate, she continually undermined her own goal as evidenced in the decisions she made while carrying out the interaction. These decisions include

- asking a rather broad question that requires no more than a yes/no answer
- not answering Claudia's request with the single word she requested
- chastising Claudia, saying that they have already studied two words
- providing a grammatical treatise in response to Claudia's request for a single lexical item
- interrupting the learner, Claudia, before she finished her sentence
- assuming she knows Claudia's complete response based on the request for a single lexical item
- never allowing Claudia to finish her sentence or her thought
- abandoning the topic and initiating another when silence followed the explanation

Leeman Guthrie concluded her analysis of the above interaction by stating that

"[it] seems clear that the issue of 'manipulation' versus 'communication' is not merely a matter of choosing between transformation drills and group discussion. Communication is an activity that requires two or more autonomous participants, one of whom may benefit from the other's skill in making the interaction succeed; but the more one participant's output is subject to another's control, the more the discourse becomes the sole creation of the more proficient individual—and that is not communication!" (1984, pp. 46–47).

She, in essence, calls for interaction not based on class discussion. How can classroom communication be structured so that the participants are autonomous? The basis for doing so is presented in Chapter 3.

SUMMARY

The purpose of presenting the six excerpts from three language lessons was to provide concrete examples of instruction about which to reflect, analyze, and synthesize. To assert that language learners are communicating is to assert that they are given opportunities to say what they mean and to work toward a mutual understanding with other interlocutors (be they instructors or other learners). All three instructors whose lessons were examined in this chapter intended to create communicative lessons, to provide learners opportunities to use the second language. Yet the results are less than desirable.

Lesson 1 actually provided learners a task during which communication took place. But when the instructor stepped in to manage the interaction, we saw very little communication among the learners. The instructor, through her questions, assumed the responsibility of ensuring that everyone comprehended and that everyone had the information they needed for a subsequent phase of the activity. Later, her impromptu discussion of the advantages and disadvantages of having a twin relied on questions and answers to promote interaction. In Lesson 2, the instructor's overwhelming linguistic output was questions; the exception was the singing contest. In going over the results of the singing contest the instructor and learners communicated. They worked toward a mutual understanding until the instructor decided to end the conversation. This instructor also engaged in gratuitous group work. She asked learners to work in groups on a task, but the groups were not held responsible for the results of the task. While the instructor in Lesson 2 curtailed communication, the instructor in Lesson 3 usurped it. She cut off the learner, assuming she knew what the learner was going to say.

A critical descriptor that cannot be applied to these instructors is *mutual*. Expressing, interpreting, and negotiating meaning is not a mutual endeavor among all the participants of these lessons. Both these instructors need to let go. Gerngroß and Puchta (1984, p. 91) refer to "letting go" as a process that requires significant changes in instructors' beliefs toward teaching, learning, and materials construction. What we first need to let go of is structuring communication around questions and answers and rather structure it to allow for expression, interpretation, and negotiation of meaning. Chapter 3 presents one way to do just that so that someone besides the instructor is communicating in the language classroom.

GAINING GREATER PERSPECTIVE

1. *Learner Interaction.* The research carried out by Brooks (1990) and Kinginger (1990) provides examples of such paired, learner-to-learner interactions. Donato (1994) also provides examples of learner-to-learner interaction, carried out in groups of three, in which the three speakers collaboratively resolve linguistic difficulties in ways reminiscent of the supportive speech between caretakers and children. Perhaps the differences lie in paired versus group interaction.

2. *Classroom Discourse.* Johnson (1995) provides an excellent and thorough examination of classroom communication. See in particular Chapter 2 on teachers' control of the patterns of communication and Chapter 6 on teacher-directed patterns of communication. Leeman Guthrie (1984, pp. 35–54) offers several other examples of how the *communication = question & answer* paradigm can get played out in classrooms. The examples illuminate how the best-intentioned instructors often subvert their own goals. In a different vein, Freeman (1992) presents and analyzes many different sessions from a high school French class. He praises the instructor he observed for her "authority over content and control over activity" (p. 58) as she constructed a non-Atlas-like classroom atmosphere.

APPLICATION ACTIVITIES

1. In Lesson 1, the instructors and learners negotiated a 15-minute time limit for cutting and pasting together their people. The instructor, however, allowed them to take 25. What are some of the possible consequences in terms of classroom management if the learners figure out that announced time limits are not adhered to?

2. Read the following description of the Atlas Complex and apply this construct to particular aspects of Lessons 1 and 2.

   "[Certain instructors] assume full responsibility for all that goes on. They supply motivations, insight, clear explanations, even intellectual curiosity. In exchange, their students supply almost nothing but a faint imitation of the academic performance that they witness. [Instructors] so thoroughly dominate the proceedings that they are cut off from what the students know or are confused about. For their part, the students form a group of isolated individuals who have no more in common than their one-to-one relationship with the same individual. While [instructors] exercise their authority through control of the subject matter and the social encounter in the classroom, they lack the power to make things happen for their students . . . [This is] the Atlas Complex" (Finkel & Monk 1983, p. 85).

   To what extent do these instructors illustrate the Atlas Complex? To answer this question, you will have to consider the following ideas extracted from Finkel and Monk's description.

   - Who is responsible for learning?
   - What do the learners supply?
   - Does the instructor know what confuses the learners?
   - What do the learners have in common?
   - How does the instructor exercise authority?
   - Does the instructor make things happen for the learners?

3. Kinginger (1995) provides a larger context for understanding why the Atlas Complex might be so pervasive in educational settings. She states,

"It was, indeed, early Utilitarians who, in the mid-nineteenth century, institutionalized a division between formal and informal learning via generalized, compulsory education. Structured to train a workforce who would willingly give up traditional practices and values in favor of wealth production through technology and industry, the public school took on many of the attributes of its parallel institution, the *factory*. Classrooms were, in fact, designed to maximize the efficiency and cost effectiveness with which knowledge is progressively dispensed in discrete measured quantities. This commodity—formal knowledge—was produced by researchers, collected by teachers, then *transmitted* to students. With the emergence of institutionalized schooling came devaluation of nonformal learning: forced separation of working and learning contexts; emphasis on the quantifiable; and, of course, the conception of the student mind as a vessel to be filled with knowledge, through the purposeful act of teaching" (1995, pp. 130–131; emphasis added).

Consider how pervasive the transmission model is in education. Can you provide examples from your own experiences? Can you provide examples of instructors who did not rely on this model?

4. Examine the following lesson and explain how the group work could be considered gratuitous.

Step 1. The bell rings. The instructor greets the class, holding in her arms worksheets that she then distributes.

Step 2. The instructor announces to the class that they have 10 minutes to complete the worksheet. This worksheet consists of a series of paragraphs. Each paragraph contains deletions, totaling about twenty. Each deletion is accompanied by multiple choices.

Step 3. At the end of 10 minutes, the instructor calls time. She directs the students to work in groups of three, coming to agreement about their answers.

Step 4. After approximately 7 minutes, the instructor brings the class's attention back to her. As a class, they go over the answers one by one, in the order they appear on the worksheet.

Step 5. The instructor reads each sentence aloud, pausing at the deletion in order to call attention to it, but continues reading to the end of the sentence. She calls upon particular students (that is, individuals do not volunteer responses) to tell which of the multiple choices appropriately completes the sentence.

Step 6. On the second item, a student supplies the correct answer. In response, the instructor explains the rules governing the particular grammatical feature exemplified in the item, i.e., comparisons using *more than* and *less than*.

Step 7. On the fifth item, a student supplies an incorrect answer. In response, the instructor explains the rules governing the particular grammatical feature exemplified in the item, i.e., conjunctions.

Step 8. On the seventh item, a student supplies a correct answer. In response, the instructor explains the rules governing the particular grammatical feature exemplified in the item, i.e., imperfect aspect.

Step 9. On the tenth item, a student supplies an incorrect answer. In response, the instructor explains the rules governing the particular grammatical feature exemplified in the item, i.e., passive constructions.

Step 10. As the instructor is finishing the explanation, the bell rings and class is dismissed.

Source: Adapted from Lee and VanPatten 1995, p. 5.

5. The singing contest is an opportunity lost for the instructor to create a negotiated communicative event. How would you set up an interaction among the learners so that they decide who sang the best?

6. Reread Excerpt 2. In analyzing the way the instructor manages the follow-up, we state that the learners are not reporting to each other but to the instructor. What can instructors do to create classroom dynamics in which learners actually report to each other? What directions do they need to be given? Would the class be seated in rows all facing the instructor? How verbally active should the instructor be?

CHAPTER 3

Developing Task-Based Activities

CHAPTER OVERVIEW

As indicated in Chapter 2, instructors who believe they are creating communicative environments in their classrooms may be going astray. They may not be creating the opportunities for learners to build toward mutual understanding. Alternatives to the *communication = question & answer* paradigm must be explored. In this chapter, we explore the basis for developing task-based activities. Crookes and Gass state that the individual authors who contributed to their edited volume adopted individual approaches to defining a *task*. They, therefore, cautioned readers that they should keep their own definition in mind as they read (1993a, p. 3). We wish only one definition to be understood by author and readers, and so we begin by developing that definition. Working from a single definition is an important first step in developing a principled approach to task-based instruction. The next step is to establish criteria for operationalizing communication in language classrooms. From there, criteria for structuring and creating task-based activities will be presented. Two task-based activities are presented in the last half of this chapter, and they are then analyzed according to the two sets of criteria presented in the first half of the chapter.

WHAT IS A TASK?

The following definition underscores an important feature of task-based instruction: Tasks provide learners a *purpose* for language use. The target language is not merely the object of manipulation as it is in drills associated with Audiolingual Methodology.

task
"(in language teaching) an activity or action which is carried out as the result of processing or understanding language (i.e., as a response). For example, drawing a map while listening to a tape, listening to an instruction and performing a command, may be referred to as tasks. Tasks may or may not involve the production of language. A

task usually requires the teacher to specify what will be regarded as successful completion of the task. The use of a variety of different tasks in language teaching is said to make language teaching more communicative . . . since it provides a purpose for a classroom activity which goes beyond the practice of language for its own sake" (Richards, Platt, & Weber 1985, p. 289).

By completing tasks, learners use language as a means to an end. The example Richards et al. provide of a task, that is, the end, is drawing a map. Other tasks include filling in a chart, filling out a form, writing a survey, conducting the survey, preparing lists, checking off items in a list, and so forth. But in all these examples, the focus is not on language forms as it was in Exercises 1 through 4 in Chapter 1.

Other definitions for *task* abound. Glass (1996) has conceptualized these definitions on a continuum from real-world context to general educational perspectives to language classroom context. He gathered the following seven definitions not only to point out their differences, but also to underscore the essential nature of a task: It is carried out with a purpose.

"A piece of work undertaken for oneself or for others freely or for some reward. Thus, examples of task include painting a fence, dressing a child, filling out a form . . . in other words, by *task* is meant the hundred and one things people *do* in everyday life, at work, at play, and in between" (Long 1985, p. 89).

". . . a piece of work or activity, usually with a specified objective, undertaken as part of an educational course, at work, or used to elicit data for research" (Crookes 1986, p. 1).

". . . instructional questions which ask, demand or even invite learners (or teachers) to perform operations in input data. The data itself may be provided by teaching material or teachers or learners. I shall term this limited set of tasks *instructional tasks*" (Wright 1987, p. 48).

". . . the notion of task used in a broad sense to refer to any structural language learning endeavor which has a particular objective, appropriate content, a specified working procedure, and a range of outcomes for those who undertake the task. *Task* is therefore assumed to refer to a range of workplans which have the overall purpose of facilitating language learning—from the simple and brief exercise type to more complex and lengthy activities such as group problem-solving simulations and decision-making" (Breen 1987, p. 23).

"One of a set of differentiated, sequenceable problem-posing activities involving learners and teachers in some joint selection from a range of varied cognitive and communicative procedures applied to existing and new knowledge in the collective exploration and pursuance of foreseen or emergent goals within a social milieu" (Candlin 1987, p. 10).

". . . a piece of classroom work which involves learners in comprehending, manipulating, producing or interacting in the target language while their attention is principally focused on meaning rather than form" (Nunan 1989, p. 10).

"A task is essentially goal-oriented: it requires the group, or pair, to achieve an objective that is usually expressed by an observable result, such as brief notes or lists, a rearrangement of jumbled items, a drawing, a spoken summary. This result should be attainable only by interaction between participants: so within the definition of the task you often find instructions [to learners] such as 'reach a consensus,' or 'find out everyone's opinion' " (Ur 1996, pp. 123–124).

The consensus is that task-based instruction views language use as a means to an end. Beyond that, variation characterizes the definitions. The following definition of task will guide the discussion in the remainder of the book. It is offered within an instructional context and is, therefore, a pedagogically logical definition of task.

"A *task* is (1) a classroom activity or exercise that has (a) an objective attainable only by the interaction among participants, (b) a mechanism for structuring and sequencing interaction, and (c) a focus on meaning exchange; (2) a language learning endeavor that requires learners to comprehend, manipulate, and/or produce the target language as they perform some set of workplans.

> **The claim that the definition of *task* that ends this section (What Is a Task?) is pedagogically logical is supported by its connections to the classroom excerpts presented in Chapter 2. An objective attainable only by the interaction among participants addresses the issue of gratuitous group work. A mechanism for structuring and sequencing interaction addresses the idea that *communication = question & answer*, the impromptu discussion, and the Poor Claudia excerpts. A focus on meaning exchange among participants addresses the ways in which instructors assume responsibility and place themselves centrally in interactions.**

AN APPROACH TO TASK-BASED INSTRUCTION

Different authors cast task-based activities in different ways. Legutke and Thomas classify Di Pietro's (1987) strategic-interaction scenarios as task-based instruction. In these scenarios, students adopt roles and negotiate their way in and out of a contrived situation. They also classify Moskowitz's (1978) suggestions for humanistic activities as task-based. In short, it appears that they consider any activity to be task-based if its purpose is not to practice language forms but to use language as a vehicle for communication, which they define as "expressing, implying and creating meaning" (1991, p. 29). That is, for them, activities are task-based simply if they go beyond practicing language for its own sake. We will propose an approach to task-based instruction that embodies the idea of language use as a means to an end, and in so doing, propose certain principles around which to develop, create, and evaluate task-based activities.

The instructor in Excerpt 6 Poor Claudia (Chapter 2) carried out what can only be termed an unsuccessful discussion. Examining the interaction between instructor and learners, we see that the learner, Claudia, had a message she wanted to convey. That is, the instructor's lack of success is not derived from class members having nothing to say on the topic, because we know Claudia intended to make a statement. The instructor's lack of success can be attributed partially to the fact that Claudia was unable to say what she wanted to since she could not recall a lexical item. The instructor's subsequent decisions also contribute to his lack of success. After the instructor's mini-lesson, Claudia and the class fell silent. When silence meets the discussion question, the desperate instructor is left to rephrase, rethink, and redirect the question(s).

This all too typical classroom scenario underscores the fundamental drawback of the *communication = question & answer* paradigm (with the possible exception of yes/no questions): The question and answer format does not provide any linguistic support for learner production. That is, learners are left to their own devices to come up with the language they need to communicate. Moreover, a class discussion that degenerates into a conversation between the instructor and the two best learners in the class can be a frustrating experience for the rest of the class. How successful is a speaking activity if only two of twenty-five class members speak? If more than five of the twenty or thirty class members are silent, then they are, in essence, principle, and practice, disenfranchised. They are not part of the instructional process, and, just as important, they may not be cognitively engaged in learning processes. Instructors clearly run the risk of having the non-speaking class members tune out if they are not part of the interaction. If these learners are not even attending to the language produced around them, then they are not engaged in language development.

If we assume that using the language is an important part of language learning (e.g., Day's 1986 edited volume of such research), we must provide activities that allow for maximal participation of each individual class member. Open-ended discussion questions are questionable, if not unreliable, pedagogical tools for promoting language development in second language learners. Among the empirical evidence for the position that open-ended discussions are less than optimal for language learning is the research of Pica and her colleagues. Pica, Kanagy, and Falodun (1993) found that open-ended discussions fostered *less* negotiation of meaning and interaction among participants than did tasks in which participants had to share information in order for the group to solve a problem or for it to come to a single decision. That such cooperative learning would yield these results is not surprising, since "students help other students within groups of four or five persons in an effort to reach goals . . . there is an interdependence established among the students in each group as they strive for the achievement of group or individual objectives" (Richard-Amato 1988, p. 193). As will be illustrated in the remainder of this chapter, task-based activities address the shortcomings inherent in a classroom dynamic born out of the restricted definition that *communication = question & answer*. Task-based activities focused on problem solving, consensus building, and interdependent group functioning not only promote the active participation of each individual class member but can be constructed in such a way as to provide learners varying degrees of linguistic support.

Criteria for Operationalizing Communication

Littlejohn and Hicks (1987, pp. 70–71) present five basic features of communication that they expect to see mirrored in the design of language tasks.

1. *Extended Discourse.* Using a language to communicate involves the speaker (or writer) in planning speech in the context of discourse (multiple, connected sentences). Language tasks should give learners experience in processing language above the sentence level.
2. *An Information Gap.* If interlocutors are in possession of the same information, then communication cannot be said to take place. A fundamental characteristic, then, of language tasks is that they require learners to share information not previously known to all participants in the task.
3. *Uncertainty.* Nonclassroom communication is unrehearsed and the discourse proceeds in a state of uncertainty. A speaker does not know beforehand what other interlocutors will say nor how they will say it. Language tasks should therefore provide learners opportunities to choose what they say and how they want to say it.
4. *Goal Orientation.* Interlocutors are conscious of some goal they wish to achieve; they hope to get something out of an interaction. A speaker does not know beforehand what the other interlocutors are going to say nor how they are going to say it. Language tasks should provide learners some purpose for communicating with each other.
5. *Real-Time Processing.* Communication unfolds and, as it does, interlocutors attend to many factors at once, spontaneously. Language tasks should reflect this spontaneity in real-time language processing.

It should be evident from the definitions of task presented earlier in the chapter that there is no one way to engage in task-based instruction or to construct task-based activities. Accordingly, the approach to task-based instruction presented here is an expansion of Lee (1995) and takes into account certain principles regarding both communication and classroom dynamics. Specifically, the approach emphasizes that

1. Communication is the expression, interpretation, and negotiation of meaning.
2. Communication requires two or more autonomous participants.
3. In the classroom, communication should privilege the learners' use of the language, not the instructor's.

Not only does the approach emphasize these dimensions of communication, it seeks to create materials that embody these principles.

Criteria for Structuring Activities

For illustrative purposes, the discussion question is used as a springboard to highlight the idea that task-based instruction represents another evolution in language teaching materials. Just as mechanical drills evolved to communicative drills to paired interaction to class discussions, class discussions can evolve toward task-based activities. In order to make this connection to the past, a series of typical discussion questions will be presented and then recast as task-based activities. The following questions guide recasting the discussion questions and serve as the basis for analyzing and discussing the structure of each activity presented.

1. *Identify a desired informational outcome.* What information is supposed to be extracted from the interaction by the learners?

   This question presupposes a purpose for having a discussion in the target language other than simply having learners speak. Whereas discussions in history, literature, and linguistics classes purport to clarify the issues, discussions in language classes generally fail to incorporate cognitive, academic goals. Discussions in language classes, as evidenced by Leeman Guthrie's instructor, generally settle for a linguistic goal.

2. *Break down the topic into subtopics.* What are the relevant subcomponents of the topic?

   The instructor that Leeman Guthrie (1984) recorded began the discussion by posing a broad question that required no more than a yes/no answer. The instructor then had to salvage the discussion by breaking it down; she asked if the French were nationalistic. I propose that a more successful approach to engaging learners in language use is to identify the subcomponents a priori and build them into the fabric of the interaction. In fact, the task-based activities presented in this chapter all lead the learners to a discussion *after* they have examined the subcomponents of the topic.

3. *Create and sequence concrete tasks for learners to do, for example, create lists, fill in charts, make tables.* What tasks can the learners carry out to explore the subcomponents?

   The paradigm that *communication = question & answer* provides language learners very little support for carrying out the interaction. The interaction depends upon them being able to access information they have stored in memory, to then encode that information linguistically (if they can), and produce it in a timely fashion. Most instructors are very uncomfortable with silence and, in the end, redirect and reformulate questions as well as answer the questions themselves. A more successful approach to engaging learners in language use is to provide them concrete tasks to carry out so that they access and retrieve the information they have stored in memory. Having retrieved the information and having it physically in front of them will engender a completely different dynamic from that of the instructor talking with the two best students in the class.

As instructional practices moved from audiolingual drills toward their communicative counterparts, many instructors described themselves as eclectic practitioners, selecting and using "what worked." They chose a variety of activity types for the sake of variety. They chose group work because group work was supposed to be good, never mind if the group work was gratuitous. Variety for variety's sake is a rather unprincipled approach to making instructional decisions. The term *eclectic*, then, should be further qualified as *principled eclecticism*. Professionals should be able to identify the principles and criteria that guide their decision making.

4. *Build in linguistic support, either lexical or grammatical or both.* What linguistic support do the learners need?

The learner Claudia (Excerpt 6 in Chapter 2) obviously had something she wanted to say on the topic of the French personality. She was not successful, however, in retrieving or encoding her thoughts in the target language. She asked for linguistic support, and what the instructor gave her was not what she asked for. That decision undermined the instructor's goal of having a discussion. A more successful approach to engaging learners in language use—one that avoids having instructors make decisions that undermine their good intentions—is to build linguistic support into the fabric of the activity.

FROM DISCUSSION QUESTIONS TO TASK-BASED ACTIVITIES

The following discussion questions probably sound familiar to most language instructors, who perhaps can picture themselves in front of their classes asking these or very similar questions.

What did you do last week? Did you play a sport? Did you read a book? Was last week an active week or was it more sedentary? How many in the class had an active week? Was last week fairly typical of your level of physical activity?

What are the best shows on television? What are the worst? Do you have favorite shows? Do shows present a positive image of Americans to Americans? What would Latin Americans, Japanese, or Egyptians think of North Americans if all they saw was your favorite TV show? How are women, minorities, Jewish people, etc., portrayed on TV?

Each set of discussion questions will now be recast in a task-based format based on the principles of communication, classroom dynamics, and activity structure outlined previously. Each activity will then be analyzed according to these same principles.

It is important to note that the two activities presented in this chapter form the basis for subsequent chapters. These activities will be expanded, modified, and adapted for higher levels of language learners in Chapter 6, for forming part of a complete language learning/teaching experience in Chapter 7, and, finally, for a variety of testing purposes in Chapters 8 and 9.

Activity A.1   What Did You Do Last Week?

The first task-based activity that serves as a data source for this treatise has been adapted from one presented in Lee and VanPatten (1995, p. 200). Activity A.1 explores leisure time activities, a very common topic found in introductory language materials. As you read over the activity, note how communication is not equated with question and answer, and how the activity structure moves learners through a series of interactional groupings: from pairs to whole class to pairs to whole class.

Step 1. Working with a partner, indicate if each activity is physically sedentary or active. You and your partner must agree on the categorization.

	SEDENTARY	ACTIVE
1. dancing at a party	☐	☐
2. riding a bike	☐	☐
3. playing video games	☐	☐
4. playing a sport	☐	☐
5. reading a book	☐	☐
6. watching TV	☐	☐
7. writing a letter	☐	☐
8. making dinner	☐	☐

Does the rest of the class agree with your categorizations of these activities?

Step 2. Add three activities to the list, preferably three that you or your partner engage in, and indicate whether or not they are sedentary.

	SEDENTARY	ACTIVE
_____	☐	☐
_____	☐	☐
_____	☐	☐

Compare your activities with those of your classmates. Do you all engage in similar activities?

Step 3. Interview your partner about what he or she did last week. Keep track of the answers because you will need them in Step 4.

MODEL: —Did you play any sports last week?
—I played tennis twice last week.

Step 4. Compare your partner's responses to the categorizations you made in Steps 1 and 2. Then use the following scale to rate your partner's week.

VERY SEDENTARY		AS SEDENTARY AS ACTIVE		VERY ACTIVE
1	2	3	4	5

Step 5. Using your evaluations of each other's level of activity, draw a class profile. Overall, to what degree was everyone's week sedentary or active?

Analyzing the Communication and Classroom Dynamics

Using the definition of communication as the expression, interpretation, and negotiation of meaning, let's analyze the communication that Activity A.1

engenders. Step 1 requires pairs of learners to negotiate a joint decision concerning the sedentary qualities of a series of leisure time activities; their task is to check off the appropriate box that reflects their decision. Then, as an entire class, they verify that they have the same evaluations. The learners follow up this whole-class interaction with another paired one in which the two learners create a list of additional activities and classify them according to the criteria of sedentary/active. They also share this list in a whole-class format. To negotiate joint decisions and share those decisions, learners must express and interpret each other's meanings; they have no choice in the matter. Subsequently, the learners interview each other about what they did last week; the interview task requires them to express, interpret, and negotiate each other's meanings particularly so in this case. Each pair of learners will construct the interview differently; the individuals decide for themselves when they have sufficient information to make the required evaluation. Finally, each individual must then rate the other's level of activity, using a scale provided, and report it to the rest of the class. In this last step, their task is to circle a number on the rating scale and report what the number is.

The activity provides autonomous participants an objective attainable only through their verbal interaction. It structures and sequences the interaction while focusing them on meaning exchange. Activity A.1 repeatedly moves learners from pairs to whole class, each time shifting the task carried out in pairs. Whereas the instructor takes the lead during the whole-class portions, the learners are continually engaged with each other; they are participating autonomously in a series of tasks. Finally, the intent of task-based activities is to privilege learners' use of language, not the instructor's. That goal is met in this activity though paired decision making, co-creating lists of activities, and interviewing each other. Although the instructor does have a series of managing functions at specific junctures between steps of the activity, the vast majority of language production comes from the learners.

Analyzing the Activity Structure

Four criteria were proposed to guide the analysis of an activity's structure and they will now be applied to Activity A.1   What Did You Do Last Week?

1. *What information are learners supposed to extract from the interaction?* Rather than limit the interaction to something such as "Get in groups and find out what others did last week," Activity A.1 adopts a particular perspective on finding out this information, which is to classify activities as sedentary or active. We look to how the activity ends in order to determine purpose. Ultimately, the learners draw a profile of the entire class. The profile motivates (in backward fashion) all the other steps in the activity.
2. *What are the subcomponents of the topic?* In order to draw a profile of the class's activity level, the learners explore a number of subcomponents of the topic. First, they are given a basis for evaluating activity; in this example, the binary option of physically active or sedentary. To draw the class profile, the learners use the framework they have been given to interview a classmate. They must extract sufficient information during the interview to carry out the evaluation. Each individual evaluation contributes to the whole.

3. *What tasks can the learners carry out to explore the subcomponents?* The tasks the learners carry out in Activity A.1 are simple yet varied. Pairs of learners categorize activities as either sedentary or active. Pairs of learners create a list of activities and then categorize them as either sedentary or active. The same pairs interview each other. Finally, individuals select a number on a rating scale that classifies the activity level of the person they interviewed. Whereas the bulk of this activity is carried out in the same pairing of learners, the task varies from step to step. After each step of the interaction, learners are reporting results to the rest of the class.

4. *What linguistic support do the learners need?* The list of activities in Step 1 certainly provides learners lexical support for the rest of the interaction. At a minimum, these activities as well as those each pair suggests for Step 2 provide the lexical basis for the interview. Moving beyond the surface, instructors might recognize that the activities listed are all presented in English as gerunds. Other languages, such as Spanish and French, would use an infinitive form, as in *running five miles* versus *correr cinco millas*. In essence, Step 1 also provides grammatical support by providing the learners the appropriate nominal form of these activities derived from verbs. Learners can use these forms to structure their interactions. For example,

Running five miles is an active activity.
Correr cinco millas es una actividad activa.

Using these activities as building blocks for grammar instruction is treated in Chapter 7.

Activity B.1   The Best Shows on TV

The second task-based activity that serves as a resource explores the types of images portrayed on television. As you read over the activity, note how communication is once again not equated with questions and answers, and how the activity structure moves learners through a series of interactional groupings: from group to whole class.

Activity B.1   The Best Shows on TV

Step 1. Form groups of four people. Your instructor will assign to each group one of the following sentences to complete. Try to come up with at least three ways to complete the sentence.

1. The best TV shows do not present women as _____.
2. The best TV shows do not present men as _____.
3. The best TV shows do not present children as _____.
4. The best TV shows do not present Jewish people as _____.
5. The best TV shows do not present people of African descent as

   _____.
6. The best TV shows do not present gays and lesbians as _____.
7. The best TV shows to not present _____ as _____.

Step 2. Present your ideas to the class and listen as the other groups present theirs. Be sure you take notes on what other groups present because you will need that information in Step 3. If you disagree with any group, be sure to say so. If you have other ideas to present, be sure to do so.

Step 3. Now that the class has characterized the treatment of people on the best shows on TV, identify programs, past and present, that fit your descriptions. How many can you come up with for each of these categories? Are TV shows better today than in the past in terms of how they present different people?

Reflective practice is a model of teacher training that has recently gained much attention. It involves a cycle. Reflective practice entails knowledge gain; that is, formally studying concepts related to learning and teaching. Knowledge gain is followed by practice or implementation: the opportunity to act on the knowledge. The actions are then analyzed. The analysis should lead to a type of synthesis that feeds into the knowledge base. Instructors gain knowledge in two ways, through formal study and by synthesizing their own applications of formal study. Knowledge growth should then affect classroom practice. This model provides the rationale for the extensive analyses of the two activities presented in this chapter.

Analyzing the Communication and Classroom Dynamics

Activity B.1 continues to operationalize communication as the expression, interpretation, and negotiation of meaning. In Step 1, groups make statements that reflect their opinions. They then share these views with other classmates in Step 2. To share opinions requires expression and interpretation. The group work required in Step 1 consists of autonomous participants in that each is linguistically equal to the others. Negotiation is encouraged by indicating to the learners that they should express their disagreement and should add to lists presented by other groups. The notetaking task should, therefore, involve not only the expression and interpretation of meaning, but also the negotiation of meaning. The final criteria for analyzing both the way communication is operationalized as well as the classroom dynamic is to determine whether the learners are given more opportunities to speak than the instructor. In Activity B.1, the instructor speaks very little outside of managing the activity. The learners express their individual opinions, share them with the class, and then suggest examples to support their opinions. Indeed, the learners' use of the language has been privileged throughout each step of the activity.

Analyzing the Activity Structure

Four criteria were proposed to guide the analysis of an activity's structure and they will now be applied to Activity B.1 *The Best Shows on TV.*

1. *What information are learners supposed to extract from the interaction?* Discussing, in the traditional sense of the word, the best shows on TV at the introductory level of language instruction probably entails nothing more than an instructor standing in front of the class asking students to name their favorite TV show. Such an interaction is quite limited for all the reasons already presented. Rather than limit the interaction, Activity B.1 provides the learners a framework and perspective for discussing the best shows on TV, that is, the treatment of groups of people. From the interaction, learners develop the criteria for naming the shows asked for in the last step.

2. *What are the subcomponents of the topic?* In order to name the best TV shows, learners must first have a common reference point. If asked to name one of the best shows on TV, someone might name National Geographic Explorer, someone else might name Sherlock Holmes Mysteries, and yet another might identify America's Most Wanted. Discussing the relationship between the three shows would prove difficult, not only conceptually but linguistically, for first-year learners. To address conceptual and linguistic concerns, the activity structure first gives learners a basis for evaluating shows. In Step 1, specific categories are identified (Item 7 is presented as an open category into which other groups such as Hispanics, Asians, working-class people, professors, etc., could be placed). These same categories are used to structure the interaction in Steps 2 and 3.

3. *What tasks can the learners carry out to explore the subcomponents?* The tasks the learners carry out in Activity B.1 are simple: (a) complete sentences; (b) present the completions; (c) note the completions of other groups; (d) add to the lists of other groups; and (e) list TV shows that meet the criteria.

4. *What linguistic support do the learners need?* Step 1 provides learners grammatical support. In English, the auxiliary *do* is a problematic structure to acquire. Additionally, English negation displays its own acquisition pattern. Learners are given the grammatical support needed to focus their production on a noun that completes the sentence. For example,

> The best shows do not present . . .
> > women as victims / sex kittens / adulteresses.
> > children as brats / smarter than adults.

The sentence structure will, however, provide learners the means to express their ideas and concepts. Languages other than English could use this activity to demonstrate the correct syntax of negative constructions as in the following Spanish examples, which also contain the preposition **a** to mark an animate object and the use of the definite article to indicate reference to membership in larger groups.

> Los mejores programas no presentan (nunca)...
> > a las mujeres como...
> > a los niños como...

SUMMARY

The chapter began with a list of definitions of *task*. The one point on which all agree is that a task provides language learners a purpose for using the language other than manipulating language forms. After examining a series of definitions, we arrived at a pedagogically logical definition to guide the remainder of the book. Our definition maintains that the activity can be accomplished only as a result of learner interaction. Also, the activity must structure and sequence the interaction. And finally, there must be a focus on meaning exchange. From this definition we moved to an approach to task-based instruction.

First we presented criteria for operationalizing communication, including extended discourse, an information gap, uncertainty, goal orientation, and real-time processing. Next we presented criteria for structuring activities, including identifying a desired informational outcome, breaking down the topic into subtopics, creating and sequencing concrete tasks, and building in linguistic support. Using these two sets of criteria, we then transformed two sets of traditional discussion questions into task-based activities. In Chapter 4, we compare the results of carrying out a whole-class discussion with the results of carrying out the task-based version of the discussion.

GAINING GREATER PERSPECTIVE

1. *Tasks.* In the broad sense that Legutke and Thomas adhere to, the following also offer suggestions for task-based activities: Moskowitz (1978), Sadow (1982), Wright et al. (1984). There are many other such resource books and a few textbooks that incorporate task-based instruction (VanPatten et al. 1996; Lee et al. 1994, 1996). One of the most cited works on task-based instruction is Nunan (1989, 1991), who offers another approach to task-based instruction.

   The justification for developing task-based materials presented in this chapter is one of privileging negotiative language use from both a quantifiable point of view and a social interaction point of view. Foley (1991) offers a psycholinguistic framework to justify task-based approaches.

2. *Social Interaction Perspective.* Brooks and Donato (1994) analyze learner discourse from a Vygotskyan perspective as opposed to the approach that quantifies the linguistic elements of communication breakdowns. Other works along this line include Brooks, Donato, and McGlone (1997), Coughlan and Duff (1994), and Donato (1994).

APPLICATION ACTIVITIES

1. Examine once again the lessons analyzed in Chapter 2. Try to construct three task-based activities from the discussions in these lessons. The first activity should address the advantages and disadvantages of having a twin. The second should address the different types of emotions involved in different types of relationships. The third activity should have the learners decide which group wins the singing contest. Be sure to use the following questions to guide your construction of the activity. For now, limit yourself to an activity that comprises only three steps.

   Guiding Questions
   a. *Identify a desired outcome.* What information are students supposed to extract from the interaction?
   b. *Break down the topic into subtopics.* What are the relevant subcomponents of the topic?

    c. *Create and sequence concrete tasks for learners to do, for example, create lists, fill in charts, make tables.* What tasks can the learners carry out to explore the subcomponents?

    d. *Build in linguistic support, either lexical or grammatical or both.* What linguistic support do the learners need?

2. After creating your three activities, analyze them using the following criteria. Is communication the expression, interpretation, and negotiation of meaning? Do the interactional groupings require two or more autonomous participants? Does the activity privilege the learners' use of the language, and not the instructor's?

3. Examine several introductory language textbooks and select an activity that is not task-based. Then recast the activity, incorporating the approach to task-based instruction outlined in this chapter. If possible, teach this activity and record the interaction in the classroom.

4. As formulated, Activity A.1 What Did You Do Last Week? incorporates what Brown and Yule (1983) refer to as interactional and transactional language use; that is, language that is used to establish social relationships as well as to transmit information or discuss content. Or as Cook describes this duality: "Language is for forming relationships with people and for interrelating with them" (1991, p. 139). How does Activity A.1 promote the development of social relationships? Do whole-class discussions permit social relations to develop or do they promote a dynamic wherein the learners only have a relationship to the instructor but not to each other?

CHAPTER 4

An Experiment
in Communication

CHAPTER OVERVIEW

In Chapter 3, discussion questions were transformed into task-based activities. In this chapter, we examine what actually happens in classrooms when an instructor carries out a whole-class discussion versus a task-based activity. The discussion and the activity cover the same content. In one interaction, the instructor asked the class questions in an attempt to get class members to talk. In another interaction, the instructor provided a task-based activity and set the class to work. Data will be presented regarding the extent of verbal participation in the two types of interaction. Data will also be presented regarding how much information learners gain and retain from these interactions.

A Summary of the Problems with Discussion Questions

In Chapter 2 we presented six classroom excerpts. Although each classroom was communicatively oriented, the instructors tended, to varying degrees, to use questions and answers as a means of structuring interaction. The following list summarizes the problems encountered in equating communication with questions and answers.

1. Few learners participate verbally in class discussions.
2. Many class discussions might best be called conversations between the instructor and a few learners rather than whole-class discussions.
3. Many class discussions might best be called linguistically lopsided in that the instructor speaks more, and more often, than any of the learners, individually or combined.
4. Instructors' questions tend to serve to extract information on a subject rather than to prompt a consideration of the subject by the class (learner-to-learner reporting or interaction is rare).
5. Linguistic roles tend to be restricted to instructors asking the questions and learners responding to them.
6. During some question and answer sessions, learner silence (or lack of response to questions) is just as much a part of the linguistic landscape as learner responses are.

7. Instructors can undermine their own goal of getting learners to speak either with (a) the question they ask, (b) the way they respond to learners' requests for help, or (c) by responding for the learners.

A Summary of the Case for Negotiative Tasks

In Chapters 1 and 3, we presented reasons why researchers and instructors emphasize negotiation. They were

1. A theory of first and second language acquisition holds that, since interactions between speakers promote comprehension, and since comprehensible input promotes acquisition, interactions promote acquisition.
2. Classroom research on negotiative tasks has consistently found that individual learners have more opportunities to use the language and more opportunities to use the language communicatively.
3. A social view of communication emphasizes negotiative language use as a principal rationale for an interaction and not as something that happens only when speakers misunderstand each other.
4. Classroom practices demonstrate that learners focus on and manipulate forms during communicative drills rather than focusing on the communicative aspects of the drill.
5. Tasks, in contrast to communicative drills or discussions, provide a purpose for language use and not just a means to manipulate language as an object. Finally, we can add to the list
6. The seven problems with discussion questions we listed in the previous section.

EXPERIMENT

Research Questions

A key argument in the research on tasks is that they increase learners' opportunities for language use. Any comparison of discussion questions and task-based activities should, therefore, examine participation patterns. What are the learners' opportunities to express, interpret, and negotiate meaning? That is, how many learners participate in discussions compared to task-based activities? Since a discussion is, by definition, the consideration of a subject, and the approach to constructing task-based activities presented in Chapter 3 emphasizes an informational outcome, any comparison of discussion questions and task-based activities should, therefore, examine how much information emerges through the two interactional formats. How much

> If you were to read an article in a professional journal that presented an experimental study, you would find a section called the *Review of Literature*. The function of this section is to present previous work that directly influences the formulation of the experiment. The first three chapters of this book provide an extended review of literature for the experiment presented in this chapter. The two summary sections at the beginning of this chapter serve to bring the content of the previous chapters back into mind. Since instruction should entail addressing the *what*, the *how*, and the *why*, you can think of a review of literature as part of the *why*.

information do learners remember immediately after the discussion and the task-based activity? Researchers are interested not only in the immediate effects of what they do, but in the long-term effects. To that end, we often measure knowledge at a later point in time. In this experiment, knowledge was measured immediately following the discussion or activity and again 1 week later. Do learners remember the information 1 week later? How much information do they remember 1 week after the discussion and the task-based activity?

Materials

The procedures and criteria developed in Chapter 3 were followed in order to create equivalent versions of a task-based activity and discussion on the topic of bilingualism and biculturalism. Both the guiding discussion questions and the task-based activity follow. The materials have been translated into English for the benefit of the reader even though the experiment was carried out in Spanish. Both the discussion questions and the task-based activity have been divided into three content-related phases: Associations, Becoming bilingual/bicultural, and Conclusions. These phases will be analyzed separately.

Guiding Discussion Questions

Phase 1. *Associations*
What do you associate with the term *bilingual*?
What do you associate with the term *bicultural*?

Phase 2. *Becoming bilingual/bicultural*
How can you become bilingual?
How can you become bicultural?

Phase 3. *Conclusions*
Do you become bilingual and bicultural in the same way?
Are they two different processes?
Can you be bicultural without being bilingual?
Can you be bilingual without being bicultural?
Is it possible to appreciate another culture without knowing its language?

Activity. Bilingual and Bicultural

Phase 1. *Associations*

Step 1. In groups of four, prepare a list of everything you associate with the terms bilingual and bicultural.

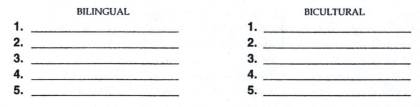

BILINGUAL	BICULTURAL
1. _____	1. _____
2. _____	2. _____
3. _____	3. _____
4. _____	4. _____
5. _____	5. _____

Phase 2. *Becoming bilingual/bicultural*

Step 2. In groups, first respond to the question, How can you become bilingual? Propose various ideas.

1. _____

2. _____

3. _____

4. _____

  Other ideas?

Step 3. Now, in groups, respond to the question, How do you become bicultural? Propose various ideas.

1. _____

2. _____

3. _____

4. _____

  Other ideas?

Phase 3. *Conclusions*

Step 4. What do you think? Do you become bilingual and bicultural in the same way? Are they two different processes? Can you be bicultural without being bilingual? Can you be bilingual without being bicultural? Is it possible to appreciate another culture without knowing its language?

Source: Adapted from Lee et al. 1996, p. 50.

Procedures

The experiment was carried out in four different third-semester Spanish classes at the University of Illinois during the last week of February 1997. Classes meet 4 days per week. For 3 of the 4 days, they cover the content of *¿Sabías que... ? Beginning Spanish,* Second Edition (VanPatten, Lee, & Ballman 1996). The textbook emphasizes all four language skills and does so in a critical-thinking framework. Activities are principally task-based and are organized into three-chapter thematic units. On the fourth day of instruction, they watch the video program *Destinos,* a Hispanic soap opera written for language learners.

Two of the four classes carried out the task-based activity, whereas the other two discussed the topic via the questions. The four classes were taught by two different instructors—the 8 A.M. and 9 A.M. classes by one and the 10 A.M. and 11 A.M. classes by another. The experimental sessions reported on here were, however, all taught by the author (a procedure followed in other research, c.f., Skehan & Foster 1997; VanPatten & Cadierno 1993). The materials were distributed such that one of each instructor's classes performed the task-based activity (9 A.M. and 11 A.M.), while the other one responded to the discussion questions (8 A.M. and 10 A.M.). All sessions were videotaped. The learners were informed before the session began that they were participating in an experiment on language learning and that their participation was completely

TABLE 4.1. Time Spent (Minutes) per Phase of Lesson

	Associations	Becoming	Conclusion	Total
Discussion 8 A.M.				
	3 bilingual 2 bicultural	2 bilingual 1 bicultural	1 bilingual/ bicultural	9
10 A.M.				
	2.5 bilingual 2 bicultural	2.5 bilingual 1 bicultural	2.5 bilingual/ bicultural	11.5
Activity 9 A.M.				
in groups	3 bilingual/ bicultural	2.5 bilingual 2 bicultural	3.5 bilingual/ bicultural	20
follow-up	3 bilingual 1.5 bicultural	1.5 bilingual 3 bicultural		
11 A.M.				
in groups	3 bilingual/ bicultural	2.5 bilingual 1.5 bicultural	1.5 bilingual/ bicultural	21.5
follow-up	4 bilingual 4 bicultural	3 bilingual 2 bicultural		

voluntary. Given the differences inherent in the two ways of structuring interaction, the various sessions required different amounts of time. The discussion in one class lasted approximately 9 minutes and in the other about 10.5 minutes. The activity took 20 minutes in one class and 22 in the other. As seen in Table 4.1, the time spent in groups generating the information was 11 and 8.5 minutes, respectively, and is approximately the same amount of time spent in front of the class eliciting the information. The overall time differences between the two formats is the time the instructor spent following up on group activities.

Immediately after the interaction, learners were given a sheet of paper that contained the following direction line (in English).

> You just talked about bilingualism and biculturalism. What I would like you to do now is summarize the information you talked about in class. I want you to write as much as you can.

They were told they were to write in English, their native language, because research has consistently shown that learners produce more in their native language than in the second language (Shohamy 1984; Lee 1986; Wolf 1993a). We chose the word *summary* for the direction line over the word *recall* because research has demonstrated that although the two words yield the same overall quantity of information, *summary* triggers more high-level ideas (Riley & Lee 1996). Learners were given another sheet of paper with similar direction lines 1 week later. Between the day the experiment took place and the follow-up a week later, no in-class discussions of bilingualism or biculturalism took place. That is, the learners had no other exposure to the topics in the intervening period.

TABLE 4.2. Participation Patterns

49

Experiment

		Number of Learners Who Spoke
Discussion		
	8 A.M.	6 of 18
	10 A.M.	5 of 24
Task-based activity		
	9 A.M.	23 of 23
	11 A.M.	23 of 23

Analysis

We are interested in determining what opportunities the learners had to express, interpret, and negotiate meaning. The specific question guiding the analysis is, How many learners participated in discussions compared to task-based activities? Table 4.2 summarizes the participation patterns across the two formats examined.

Whereas one-fifth to one-third of the learners verbally participated in the discussions, all learners verbally participated in the task-based activities.

Participation During the Discussion

In the first class, only six of the eighteen learners participated verbally. Two of the six participated in multiple segments of the lesson, which means that only these two people received any sort of extended speaking practice. In the second of the discussion classes, only five learners participated verbally. Three of the five participated in multiple phases of the discussion. (A transcript of the second class's discussion is included with the Application Activities for this chapter.) Interestingly, the whole-class discussion turned into a conversation between the researcher and two particular learners who had personal experiences relevant to the topic. The other learners did not participate verbally, although at certain points in the lesson, murmuring could be heard and heads were seen nodding.

The following is a translation and transcription of the 8 A.M. session. The original interaction took place in Spanish; italicized words were spoken in English, not Spanish. As you read the transcription, note the differences in participation across Phases 1 and 2. During Phase 1, several learners answered at the same time, as designated by the symbol ss. They either murmur consent in line 2 or give one- or two-word answers as in lines 6 and 8. But the participation pattern in Phase 1 is principally characterized as an exchange between the instructor and two learners. The first, s1, began to speak in line 12 and the second, s2, in line 24. The instructor switched back to s1 in line 41 and then back to s2 in line 45. Just as we have seen in other excerpts of *communication = question & answer*, the instructor asked the questions and the learners answered them. Moreover, the learners did not at any time interact with each other, only with the instructor.

8 A.M. Discussion

Phase 1: Associations

1. I: Something that I want to discuss with you today is bilingualism. Bilingualism. All of you study Spanish. Do you want to be bilingual? Bilingual English-Spanish?

2. SS: [*General murmuring of consent.*]

3. I: Who can tell me what it means to be bilingual? What does the word mean? What's the definition of bilingual?

4. SS: [*No answer. 5-second pause.*]

5. I: Is it a person who speaks only one language?

6. SS: No.

7. I: Three languages?

8. SS: No, two.

9. I: Two. Two. It is a person who speaks two languages. When I say the word "bilingual" what do you think about? Immediately. What do you associate with the term bilingual?

10. SS: [*No answer. 5-second pause.*]

11. I: What people? What things?

12. S1: My mother is bilingual.

13. I: Your mother is bilingual? What languages does she speak?

14. S1: English, Spanish, *Polish.*

15. I: She is trilingual. Is your mother from a Hispanic background?

16. S1: Yes.

17. I: What country is she from?

18. S1: Mexico.

19. I: Is your father also bilingual?

20. S1: No, Dad Chicago.

21. I: Your dad is from Chicago, but there are a lot of bilinguals in Chicago. A lot!

22. S1: My dad *Ireland.*

23. I: Your dad is from Ireland? I am, too. Are there others in the class who know someone who is bilingual?

24. S2: My mother is also bilingual.

25. I: Yes? What languages does she speak?

26. S2: English, Spanish.

27. I: Spanish. What country is she from?

28. S2: From Puerto Rico.

29. I: Ah. Puerto Rico. It is a very, very pretty island. Have you visited Puerto Rico before?

30. S2: Yes.

31. I: In your home, do you speak Spanish or English?

32. S2: Both.

33. I: Your father is also bilingual?

34. S2: He understands but doesn't speak.

35. I: Spanish is not a secret language, then. Your father can understand it. [*To the class.*] What else do you associate with bilingual? What do you think about? [*5-second pause.*] I have another word. Bicultural. Bicultural. If bilingual means that a person speaks two languages, what does it mean to be bicultural? [*5-second pause, then to s2.*] Is your mother bicultural?

36. s2: No.

37. I: No? She does not have two cultures?

38. s2: Yes she has two cultures. I have two cultures. I am bicultural.

39. I: Are you bilingual?

40. s2: A little.

41. I: You have two cultures but your mother only has one. That is interesting. It is interesting. [*To s1.*] In your case, do you think your mother is bicultural or is she only bilingual?

42. s1: She is only bilingual not bicultural.

43. I: No? She is bilingual. Why do you say she is not bicultural? Does she not have contact with Mexican culture?

44. s1: Her parents, not either.

45. I: Your grandparents are not bicultural. [*To s2.*] Your grandparents. Do they live in Puerto Rico or in the United States?

46. s2: Puerto Rico.

47. I: In Puerto Rico. Are they bicultural?

48. s2: No.

49. I: Monocultural?

50. s2: Yes.

> **Luck can be defined as unforeseen or unpredictable good fortune. Luck prevailed in that two members of the class had personal experience with the topics of bilingualism and biculturalism *and* that those two members were willing to share their experiences. Sometimes those with relevant personal experiences do not share them.**

The participation pattern that characterizes Phase 2 is a bit different from that of Phase 1. In the transcript that follows, four learners volunteered ideas on how to become bilingual or bicultural, whereas only two individuals spoke during Phase 1. Moreover, the exchange between s4 and the instructor between lines 56 and 65 showed that negotiation of meaning can and does take place during discussions. The issue is *how many* opportunities there are for negotiation to take place.

Phase 2: Becoming bilingual/bicultural

51. I: Let's see. You all study Spanish, true? And, it is possible for you to become bilingual. Yes? It is possible for you to become bilingual. I want to know . . . I want you to propose ideas. How can you become bilingual? How? I want to create a list. How can you become bilingual? Number 1, for example. [*7-second pause.*]

52. s3: Talk with different people who speak Spanish.

53. I: Yes, good idea. Good idea. That is, look for opportunities to practice Spanish. What else? [*5-second pause.*] This is a good way. What other ways? [*5-second pause.*] Reading? Do you think reading articles in magazines helps you to be bilingual?

54. ss: [*Some nodding in agreement.*]

55. I: Yes? Some say yes.

56. s4: Works.

57. I: What?

58. s4: Works.

59. I: Working.

60. s4: Working in the United States.

61. I: Working in the United States.

62. s4: Working for bilingual people.

63. I: Working for bilingual people or working for monolingual people.

64. s4: Yes, in the government.

65. I: Working for the government. Yes. The federal government. The state government. There are a lot of jobs that require someone to be bilingual. Now, a more difficult question. How do you become bicultural? If you can become bilingual by speaking, reading, and working, how do you become bicultural?

66. s5: Visit countries.

67. I: Very good. Visit other countries. That is, have personal contact with other cultures. Other ways?

68. s6: Lives in another country.

69. I: Very good. Live in another country or other countries. Do you know how many countries in the world are Spanish-speaking? [*5-second pause.*] More than thirty. More than thirty. Other comments.

In contrast to Phases 1 and 2, no individual learners spoke during Phase 3. The class murmured its consent in line 71 but did not contribute any specific information to the conclusion.

Phase 3: Conclusion

70. I: Oh, one more question. Is it possible to be bilingual without being bicultural?

71. ss: [*Several murmurs of yes.*]

72. I: Yes, because we have some cases. We have some cases. Good. Good. Other comments?

73. ss: [*No response.*]

Participation During the Task-Based Activity

As the videotape clearly shows, all learners verbally participated in their groups. Given the way each phase of the activity was followed up, certain learners spoke on behalf of their groups and this is designated by the symbol G. Learners who spoke on their own behalf are designated with the symbol s. During Phases 1 and 2, learners only spoke on behalf of their groups. In gathering the products of group interaction, each of the six group representatives spoke multiple times, as is shown in Table 4.3.

The following transcript of the instructor's and learners' speech during group reporting helps demonstrate the nature of the whole-class interaction and the learners' contributions to the content of the discussion. The most dramatic contrast between this transcript and the discussion is how much more content and information are elicited through the tasks. Whereas the association phase of the 8 A.M. discussion yielded two interesting personal examples of bilingual/bicultural parents, the association phase of the 9 A.M. activity yielded at least seventeen different ideas.

TABLE 4.3. Number of Times Group Representative Spoke During 9 A.M. Activity

	Phase 1	Phase 2
G1	2	3
G2	4	4
G3	6	4
G4	3	4
G5	3	3
G6	6	3

9 A.M. Task-Based Activity

Phase 1: Associations

1. I: I have here a worksheet to distribute. Good. First, I want you to divide into groups of four, groups of four people. Here we have four, and four. Divide yourselves into four people. [*5-second pause.*] Instead of having a group of five, we can have three here. OK. As a group, as a group I want you to do Step 1. OK. You have to prepare two lists. Three minutes. You have three minutes to do Step 1.

[*Groups work for 3 minutes. Instructor monitors groups, answers questions, supplies lexical items.*]

    I: [*After 2 minutes.*] You have one more minute.

    [*1 minute later.*] OK, let's see. Let's see what things you associate first with bilingual, with this term. What do you associate with the term bilingual? OK. You, one thing, one thing that you have on your list.

2. G1: Difficult.
3. I: Difficult. It is difficult to be bilingual. OK. And you, one thing.
4. G2: Speak more than one language.
5. I: Speak more than one language. Ah hah. It is the definition. Another thing.
6. G3: Accents and different verbs.
7. I: Ah hah. Accents and different verbs. Very good. This group.
8. G4: Immigrant.
9. I: OK. Immigrant or immigrants. OK. And here.
10. G5: A worldly.
11. I: A what?
12. G5: A worldly, *worldly.*
13. I: OK. Someone who knows the world. Very good. And here, this group.
14. G6: The professor.
15. I: The professor. OK. It is preferable that the professor be bilingual to teach Spanish. Yes. OK. Another thing from your list?
16. G6: Bicultural?
17. I: No, bilingual.
18. G6: Restaurants.
19. I: Bilingual restaurants. OK. [*Points to next group.*]
20. G5: Intelligence.

21. I: Intelligence. Another? This group.
22. G4: Ambassadors.
23. I: An ambassador. It is preferable that they be bilingual but it is not so in reality. [*Points to next group.*]
24. G3: Language.
25. I: Language. What else? Do you have another thing?
26. G3: No.
27. I: No? You do not have another thing to add? OK and you. Another one.
28. G2: Intelligent.
29. I: OK. Whatever group has something on their list that has not already been mentioned. Do you have something, something that we have not mentioned up till now?
30. G6: A doctor.
31. I: A doctor. Ah hah. There are bilingual doctors. Another thing.
32. G3: The radio.
33. I: Yes, there are bilingual programs on the radio. Something else? Bicultural. Let's look at bicultural. I want to start with this group. [*Points to G4.*] What do you associate with bicultural?
34. G4: Customs.
35. I: Customs, very good. And here.
36. G5: Fun. [**Diversión** in Spanish.]
37. I: Fun? Not diversity? [**Diversidad** in Spanish.]
38. G5: Diversity.
39. I: OK. La diversión is something else. And you, what do you have?
40. G6: The university.
41. I: The university as a bicultural environment. It could be. What do you have under bicultural?
42. G1: Cities.
43. I: Ah hah. They say that the city of Chicago has many cultures. Many. What do you have under bicultural?
44. G2: To have more than one background.
45. I: OK, to have more than one background, various backgrounds, various influences on a person. You?
46. G3: Food.
47. I: Food. They say food represents a culture. Good, whatever group. What do you have on your list that has not yet been mentioned? Yes.
48. G6: Work.
49. I: Work.
50. G3: Music and parties.
51. I: Music and parties.
52. G2: Family.
53. I: Family. All these are representative of a culture. Anything else? No.

During Phase 2 of the discussion, four learners spoke and offered five ideas for becoming bilingual/bicultural. During Phase 2 of the task-based activity, multiple groups spoke multiple times and offered at least fourteen different ideas on how to become bilingual/bicultural. We do have an example of negotiation that results from communication breakdown in lines 91 and 92. A group uses the Spanish **cansar** meaning *to tire of* as opposed to the graphemically similar **casar** (*to marry*) or **casarse** (*to get married.*).

Phase 2: Becoming bilingual/bicultural

54. I: Now, I want you to continue working on the activity. This time on Step 2, on Step 2. What you have to do in Step 2 . . . again you have to prepare a list. You have to propose. Propose? Give ideas. How can you become bilingual? What do you have to do? All of you. What do you have to do to become bilingual? OK. I will give you 3 minutes.

[Explains *to become* to G4, which is **llegar a ser** in Spanish. Two minutes go by.]

Good. It seems that everyone is almost finished. Let's see again. How can you become bilingual? Do you want to give me two ideas this time?

55. G6: Knows two languages and studying.

56. I: Studying. Yes, a very good idea. To know two languages it is necessary to study. And this group. Two of the ideas you have.

57. G5: Working with other people.

58. I: Yes, working with other bilingual people. Yes. Another?

59. G5: Living in another country.

60. I: Living in another country. Uh huh. Very good way. This group, two ideas you have.

61. G4: We talk a lot with another person. We travel to another country.

62. I: Talking with another person and traveling. What do you have?

63. G3: Taking more classes.

64. I: Taking more classes in Spanish or French or whatever. Spanish preferably. Another idea that has not been mentioned?

65. G3: No.

66. I: Do you have something that has not yet been mentioned?

67. G2: Yes.

68. I: Yes? What is it?

69. G2: You talk with other friends that to speak another language.

70. I: Uh huh. OK. And you, do you have something that has not been mentioned?

71. G1: Listening to a tape.

72. I: Listening to tapes or checking out videos. For example, Blockbuster has various videos in Spanish. These are very good ideas. You have very good ideas about how to become bilingual. OK. Now I want you to work on Step 3. This time you have to think about how to become bicultural. How can you become bicultural? Three minutes again.

[Monitors groups. Gives the lexical item *to marry*. Two and a half minutes go by.]

Are you ready to share lists? OK. Let's see. You. Can you give me two ideas you have about becoming bicultural?

73. G1: Participate bicultural activities.

74. I: Attend bicultural activities or participate in such activities. Very good.

75. G1: Live with another family.

76. I: Live with another family. Uh huh. Very good. Two ideas.

77. G2: Visit the homes of friends from different parts. Live in another country.

78. I: OK. Live in another country. For how long?

79. G2: Many months. More than six.

80. I: More than six months. OK. Do you have different ideas?

81. G3: Study the history of the culture.

82. I: Study the history of the culture in order to know something, something very definite about the culture. And?

83. G3: Live in a cosmopolitan city.

84. I: Live in a cosmopolitan city. Very good. A city that has many cultures. And do you have ideas that have not yet been mentioned?

85. G4: Visit other countries.

86. I: Visit and not live?

87. G4: No.

88. I: No? OK.

89. G4: Go to museum.

90. I: Ah. Go to a museum, to museums. In many big cities, in Chicago and also New York, there are museums, museums specifically dedicated to Hispanics, for example. And do you have other ideas?

91. G5: To tire of with another person who has another culture. [**Cansar** in Spanish.]

92. I: To tire of, no. To be tired is another thing. Get married? [**Casarse** in Spanish.] Marry someone from another culture or to have a girlfriend or boyfriend from another culture. That is a good way to begin to appreciate another culture. And do you have something different?

93. G6: Study other culturals.

94. I: Study them.

95. G6: And he lives with a person from another culture.

96. I: It is not necessary to get married. You can simply live with another person, with another family. It seems that it is important to have contact, important to have contact with another person. OK.

The two concluding phases show many contrasts. During the discussion, the learners only murmured their agreement, whereas during the activity, they were somewhat more vocal. The learners more clearly vocalized their agreement. Whereas no learner spoke during the conclusion of the discussion, five learners spoke during the conclusion of the activity.

Phase 3: Conclusion

97. I: Now I have some questions for you. OK? Questions. You have to offer me some opinions, some opinions, OK? Is it possible, is it possible to be bilingual without being bicultural?

98. SS: Yes.

99. I: You say yes?

100. S1: Maybe.

101. I: Maybe? You say yes. How many of you say yes? There were many people. [*Show of hands.*] What are some of your reasons? Who can offer me reasons? Why can you be bilingual without being bicultural? Sir.

102. s2: [*Inaudible.*]

103. I: Yes, you are right. It is a real case. A real case. A person can understand a language without having visited another country. Other reasons because there are many who have this opinion.

104. s3: [*Inaudible.*]

105. I: So you believe that someone could be bicultural without being bilingual? How many of you believe that this is possible? To be bicultural without being bilingual? Other cases? Are there other cases that you can offer me to support these two opinions? You said maybe.

106. s4: Nee . . . he needs. I don't know *knowledge.*

107. I: Sabiduría. Conocimiento. Conocimiento.

108. s4: Knowledge of the culture. I don't know. The culture. All he does not understand, not understand the language. All. The words and he does not know the culture.

109. I: Uh huh. Is there someone here . . . Do you know bilingual people who are not bicultural? Or on the contrary, do you know bicultural people who are not bilingual?

110. s5: Yes. I am bicultural.

111. I: What are the two cultures?

112. s5: *Norwegian* and *American.*

113. I: Norwegian culture and U.S. culture.

114. s5: Yes but I do not speak *Norwegian.*

115. I: Do your mother and your father speak Norwegian?

116. s5: Yes, mother.

117. I: Uh huh. here we have a very specific case here in the class. Is there something else you want to comment on about bilingualism and biculturalism?

118. ss: [*No response.*]

119. I: Very good.

Content Remembered Immediately After Interaction

As the previous discussion of participation patterns indicates, many more ideas emerged during the activity than during the discussion. As stated at the outset of the chapter, a *discussion* is defined as the consideration of a subject by a group. Also, the approach to constructing task-based activities presented in Chapter 3 emphasizes an informational outcome. We, therefore, posed a research question: How much information do learners remember immediately after the discussion and the task-based activity? Two raters independently analyzed each of the summary protocols for two things: the number of ideas present in the protocol that emerged during the interactions and the number of these ideas remembered correctly. Each correct idea received a score of 1. Information that was not part of the interaction was not counted and incorrect information was not counted. Interrater reliability was .94.

In each of the following tables, the ideas remembered are both totaled and distributed among the three phases of the discussion/activity. As can be seen in Table 4.4 and demonstrated statistically in Table 4.5, learners who participated in the activity recalled much more than those who participated in the discussion (9.7 versus 5.1 ideas). These differences stem from Phases 1 and 2 of

TABLE 4.4. Average Number of Ideas Remembered, Standard Deviations, and Standard Errors Immediately Following Interaction

	Discussion	Activity
Phase 1	2.1	4.7
SD	1.9	3.8
SE	.285	.557
Phase 2	1.6	3.8
SD	2.0	2.9
SE	.310	.432
Phase 3	1.4	1.2
SD	1.2	1.4
SE	.184	.199
Total	5.1	9.7
SD	2.7	5.3
SE	.411	.782
N	42	46

TABLE 4.5. Test of Significant Differences Between Discussion and Activity

	Difference	Critical Difference
Phase 1	2.622	1.281*
Phase 2	2.118	1.077*
Phase 3	.189	.544
Total	4.575	1.809*

*Significantly different at $p < .05$ level.

TABLE 4.6. Number of Learners Who Remembered Any Information

	Discussion	Activity
Phase 1	31 = 73.8%	44 = 95.7%
Phase 2	22 = 52.4%	37 = 80.4%
Phase 3	33 = 78.6%	27 = 58.7%
Overall	39 = 92.9%	46 = 100%
N	42	46

the lessons, but not Phase 3. As the transcripts of the lessons show, very little content was generated as part of the conclusion of the discussion/activity and, so, very little information is remembered. The numbers in Table 4.6 show us that overall most learners were paying attention during discussions. While 95% of them remembered some aspect of the discussion, particular phases of the lesson seemed more memorable than others. All learners participating in the activity remembered some aspect of the interaction. The percentage of people who remembered information from Phases 1 and 2 is much higher among the activity people than among the discussion people. Interestingly, a greater percentage of the discussion people remembered information from Phase 3. Overall, then, the task-based activity yielded more information remembered by more people.

TABLE 4.7. Average Number of Ideas Remembered 1 Week Following Interaction

	Discussion	Activity
Phase 1	1.2	2.5
SD	1.1	2.1
SE	.178	.345
Phase 2	1.0	2.7
SD	1.4	2.7
SE	.214	.438
Phase 3	.8	.7
SD	.8	1.0
SE	.118	.160
Total	2.9	5.9
SD	1.6	3.3
SE	.255	.535
N	41	38

TABLE 4.8. Test of Significant Differences 1 Week Following Interaction

	Difference	Critical Difference
Phase 1	1.303	.758*
Phase 2	1.757	.951*
Phase 3	.070	.393
Total	2.990	1.154*

*Significantly different at $p < .05$ level.

Content Remembered 1 Week Later

One week later, learners once again summarized what they could remember of what took place in class. Due to absences, the total number of participants is different across the two data-gathering sessions. The results are exactly the same 1 week later as they were immediately following the class session. As can be seen in Table 4.7 and demonstrated statistically in Table 4.8, learners who participated in the activity recalled much more than those who participated in the discussion (5.9 versus 2.9 ideas). For both the discussion and the task-based activity we see a loss of information, which is of course expected. These differences stemmed from Phases 1 and 2 of the lessons, but not Phase 3. The numbers in Table 4.9 show us that overall most learners were paying attention during discussions. While 90% of them remembered some aspect of the discussion, particular phases of the lesson seemed more memorable than others. The second phase, about becoming bilingual or bicultural, yielded the lowest number of people recalling information (39%). Almost all learners participating in the activity remembered some aspect of the interaction (97%). The

The *what,* or the content of the class sessions, was kept as similar as possible in this experiment. Both sets of classes were asked to associate about bilingualism and biculturalism and to suggest ways of becoming bilingual and bicultural. The *how,* or the way(s) in which the content was acted upon, varied. That variation brought about different results and outcomes.

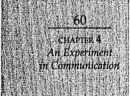

TABLE 4.9. Number of Learners Who Remembered Any Information 1 Week Later

	Discussion	Activity
Phase 1	24 = 58.5%	32 = 84.2%
Phase 2	16 = 39.0%	26 = 68.4%
Phase 3	26 = 63.4%	18 = 47.4%
Overall	37 = 90.2%	37 = 97.4%
N	41	38

percentage of people who remembered information from Phases 1 and 2 is much higher among the activity people than among the discussion people. Interestingly, a greater percentage of the discussion people remembered information from Phase 3. Overall, then, the task-based activity allowed more people to remember more information 1 week later than the discussion did.

The transcripts make it evident that more ideas came out during the activity than during the discussion and that did influence the results. There simply was more information to remember from the activity. That unequal amounts of information emerged demonstrates that discussions and activities are unequal ways to structure materials.

SUMMARY

Phase 1 Associations took 5 minutes to carry out in the 8 A.M. whole-class discussion, during which time only two learners talked about their bilingual and bicultural parents. The total number of ideas expressed was four. The rest of the class seemed very reluctant to speak as evidenced by no response to the question in line 3, What is the definition of bilingual? The instructor redirected the question in line 5, changing it from open-ended to yes/no. Phase 1 took 4.5 minutes in the 10 A.M. whole-class discussion, during which four learners offered four ideas. During the task-based activity, groups of learners were given 3 minutes to create a list of associations; the worksheet they were given was numbered from 1 to 5. These worksheets were collected at the end of the class period and they showed that all groups wrote five associations. So, in 3 minutes' time, every learner was exposed to five associations. The follow-up to the group task served potentially to expose the whole class to even more associations.

Not only did the task-based activity distribute participation more evenly, it engendered more content more efficiently. An interesting question remains for future investigation: Do the nonverbal participants in a discussion make mental associations or do they only listen to what others say? The summary data suggest that they listened to their fellow classmates, but did not elaborate on or create other associations. Future research could more directly address this question.

Any time a discussion yields little or no participation, an instructor is left wondering if the learners have anything to say on the topic or if the topic is too difficult for that level of learner to discuss. The 8 A.M. discussion got off to a slow start. Was it possible that the learners really did not have anything to say about the topic of bilingualism/biculturalism? The learners in the 10 A.M. discussion demonstrated that the topic was not problematic; they had something to say about bilingualism/biculturalism. The different responses between the two discussion classes underscore how unreliable discussion questions can be as a pedagogical tool for structuring materials and interaction. The same questions and topic might or might not yield good responses from learners. The variable nature of a whole-class discussion can also be seen in the different participation patterns across the three phases of the discussion in the 8 A.M. class. Even though the structure of the phases was identical (i.e., the instructor asked questions), participation varied from two learners in Phase 1 to four learners in Phase 2 to no individual learner responding in Phase 3. The performance of the two groups carrying out the task-based activity was much more uniform. The task-based activity clearly provided a needed mechanism for structuring and sequencing interaction. It is not the case that learners have nothing to say. Rather, they benefit greatly from having the support through which to express themselves.

An important question remains unanswered in this experiment, and it has to do with how much time learners spent on the discussion and the activity. The discussions lasted only 10 minutes, whereas the activities required 20. Is the difference in how much information is remembered due to how much time was spent on learning? It remains for future research to construct a set of discussion questions and a task-based activity that are then carried out in the same amount of time. That is, time must be held constant and not allowed to vary from one format to another.

Ur (1996) reports that she compared learner performance and reception of a discussion and a task-based activity. (She provides little detail on the comparison and so little is offered here.) Since she did not use a task-based version of the discussion questions as in the present study, her comparison is not quite as direct. She found that the task-based activity scored higher on the following criteria: There was more talk, more even participation, more motivation, and more enjoyment. The data presented in this chapter concur that there was more talk and more even participation as the activity unfolded. Additionally, the data allow us to conclude that more information/content was remembered, not only immediately after completing the task, but also 1 week later. In sum, learners not only used more language but also retained more information from task-based interactions than from whole-class discussions.

Perhaps because the task-based activity generated more content than the discussion, learners remembered and retained more content. Far more learners participated verbally in the activity than in the discussion, but the nonverbal learners in discussions did seem to be paying attention. It is important, therefore, to evenly distribute the opportunities to verbalize. Ur concludes, "Thus, as a generalization, it is probably advisable to base most oral fluency activities on tasks" (1996, p. 124). The data presented in this chapter corroborate her opinion.

GAINING GREATER PERSPECTIVE

1. *Research on Tasks.* Doughty and Pica (1986) demonstrated that negotiative tasks elicit more of the verbal behaviors associated with language acquisition than nonnegotiative tasks. This article is highly readable and serves as a point of departure for appreciating how far the field has moved in a decade. Pica, Kanagy, and Falodun (1993) compare open-ended questions with negotiative tasks and come to conclusions similar to those in this chapter.
2. *Native Language Use During Group Work.* Without monitoring and training, learners often revert to their native language during group work (only, of course, if they share a common language). How do they use their native language? Brooks, Donato, and McGlone (1997) seem to find that the high school learners they studied used their common native language to figure out the task demands, but then used the second language to carry out the task.

APPLICATION ACTIVITIES

1. During both the discussion and the activity, the instructor repeated the information the students offered. What are some reasons for the instructor to do that so consistently? Is it mere repetition or is there also expansion?
2. During the activity, the instructor chose to have each group offer one or two of the ideas they had listed. What are some of the other options available for having groups share the results of their work? Are any of these options better? Would any of these options have made the group work more or less gratuitous (see Chapter 2, Excerpt 2)?
3. Many instructors fear that they will give up or lose control of their classes if they allow learners to work in groups. How does this instructor exercise control and authority over the classroom interaction? What techniques does the instructor use? What roles does the instructor play?
4. The transcript of the second class's discussion follows. Compare it to the first class's discussion for the number of different ideas the learners present. Which class presents more information, or are they roughly equivalent? Is it accurate to say that the two students in the first class who offered personal examples "carried" the discussion? Is it accurate to say that they "saved" the discussion? Does anyone "carry" or "save" the discussion in the second class?

10 A.M. Class Session Discussion

Phase 1: Associations
   1. I: I am going to tell you a word and I want to know everything that you associate with this word. Ready? The word is "bilingual." What do you associate with "bilingual"?
   2. S1: Two languages.
   3. I: Two languages. Two languages. What else?

4. s2: English/Spanish.
5. i: English/Spanish. Uh huh. Especially in the dictionary, the bilingual dictionary you have. What else?
6. s1: Education.
7. i: Education. There is this phenomenon of bilingual education in this country. Very good. What else? Do you associate the term with certain people, for example, or not?
8. s3: Yes.
9. i: Yes? For example, anyone in particular?
10. s3: Persons is their parents a-a-are from another country. Fir-first generation here.
11. i: Yes. The first generation of a family often is bilingual. The second and third, sometimes not. Then if the parents are from other countries, bilingualism is also associated with immigration. The family, immigration, education, two languages, what else? English/Spanish. What else?
12. s4: A morning class.
13. i: A morning class but at a very convenient hour. Yes. I have another term for you. Another idea and I want to know what you associate with this word. It is "bicultural." Not bilingual, but bicultural. What do you associate with that term, with bicultural?
14. s1: Two countries.
15. i: Two countries. Uh hmm. What else?
16. s1: A life in your house and [*Inaudible.*]
17. i: Differences?
18. s1: Yes.
19. i: The home culture and the out of the home culture. What else? [*5-second pause.*] Do you associate food with biculturalism?
20. ss: [*General murmuring.*]
21. i: Yes? Other things?
22. s3: Someone they have parents from two countries, different ones.
23. i: Oh. For example, one parent is from the United States and the other is from Mexico, for example. The parents represent two different cultures. OK.

Phase 2: Becoming bilingual/bicultural

24. i: Umm, now. I have something else for you. How can you, in the future, how can you become bilinguals? How can you become bilingual? What can you do to be, to become bilingual? What are some ideas? What can you propose to me?
25. s1: Bilingual was very important for communication.
26. i: Yes. Bilingualism is important for communication. Uh huh. But how can you, what can you do to be bilingual? What can you do to become bilingual?
27. s3: Take a lot of Spanish.
28. i: Ah, very good. Very good answer. Take classes. Take classes. This is one way to become bilingual. Formally study the language. Other ways that do not have to do with school?
29. s5: You go to the, to the country of the language.

30. I: To me the idea seems very good. Go to where this language is spoken. It is a very good idea. A very good way. Other ways? [*5-second pause.*] I imagine that it is a little expensive to go to live in another country but . . . What else can you do?

31. s1: Talk with people of other languages.

32. I: Talk to bilingual people. There are a lot of bilinguals here in Champaign/Urbana. You can have contact with these people. Something else? [*4-second pause.*] Now I have another question, perhaps a little more difficult. OK. How can you become bicultural? One thing is to know two languages, another thing is to be bicultural. What ideas can you propose to me? How can you become bicultural? [*9-second pause.*]

33. s1: I do not understand the question.

34. I: OK. We have three ideas about becoming bilingual. Go to a country, study the language, another one that I do not remember. Now I want to know what can you do to be bicultural people? To be a person with two cultures. [*5-second pause.*]

Phase 3: Conclusion

35. I: I have one more question. Do you believe, and I want to see hands, do you believe that a person can be bilingual without being bicultural? That is, a person can speak two languages but the person does not have two cultures. How many believe it is true? [*Raise hands.*] Many, many. Why do you believe this?

36. s5: A person studies the language in his own country and not go to another country.

37. I: That's it. If someone studies the language without having contact with the culture. It seems to me that the person could be bilingual without being bicultural. Uh huh. Other reasons?

38. s3: Someone can learn only the language in his school, school, and not have so-someone culture than the language.

39. I: If you do not have contact with people who represent the culture and if you only have contact in school, yes, this can be the result. Yes?

40. s2: My mother is bilingual and was in two culturals but she does not practice two culturals.

41. I: Your mother is bilingual? And you say she is bicultural or not?

42. s2: She does not practice two but knows two.

43. I: She does not practice the two cultures. What are the two cultures?

44. s2: Spanish and *Japanese.*

45. I: Japanese. The Spanish culture and the Japanese culture.

46. s2: And very different.

47. I: They are two different cultures, very different. Anything else?

5. The transcript of the second class's task-based activity follows. Compare it to the first class's completion of the task. How many different ideas do the learners themselves present? Are the two task-based activities more similar to each other than the two discussions are to each other?

Phase 1: Associations

1. I: You need to work in groups of four. What I want you to do right now is, what I want you to do is divide yourselves into groups of four. Divide yourselves into groups of four. Here, a group of four. A group of four. Here, four. One, two, three, four. You can work here, OK? One, two, three. One, two, three, four, five, six. Six groups of four. Good. OK. I want you, in groups, to do Step 1, Step 1. What you have to do in Step 1 is create two lists. You have to create two lists and you have 3 minutes. Three minutes to prepare two lists. Good. [During the group work, the instructor monitors groups, answers procedural questions, provides lexical support.]

    [*After 2 minutes.*] You only have one more minute. One more minute.

    [*1 minute later.*] We are going to share the lists. We are going to share the lists. We are going to verify what everyone has to contribute to the discussion. OK. First I want to talk about bilingualism. I want to know what you have on your lists. OK, here. This group. One thing. One thing only. One thing only that you have on the list that you associate with "bilingual."

2. G1: Speaks two languages.
3. I: Speaking two languages. Very good. That is the definition. And this group. You. One thing.
4. G2: Studying.
5. I: Studying a lot. One has to study a lot in order to become bilingual. And you?
6. G3: *Interpreters.*
7. I: Interpreters? Ah hah. Interpreters are definitely bilinguals. What do you have?
8. G4: Teachers.
9. I: Teachers, professors. Ah hah, ah hah. And you here?
10. G5: *Exchange* students.
11. I: Exchange.
12. G5: Exchange.
13. I: Exchange students. Yes, yes. Here at this university we have a lot of exchange students. They come from their countries. They are bilingual. Good. And you, one thing.
14. G6: Understanding two languages.
15. I: Understanding two languages. OK. Speaking two languages, understanding two languages, too. Let's see. What do you have on the list that has not yet been mentioned? Under bilingual.
16. G6: *Foreign.*
17. I: Something or someone from, from abroad. OK, another thing. One more thing.
18. G6: Reading.
19. I: Reading. OK.
20. G6: Writing, speaking.

21. I: The four skills. OK. Very good. And you, do you have something that has not been mentioned?

22. G5: People.

23. I: People. OK, yes. Good. People in particular? Famous people?

24. G5: People people.

25. I: People people. And not animals. And not animals. OK. You, do you have anything that has not already been mentioned?

26. G4: More parties and festivities.

27. I: Bilinguals have more holidays and festivities to celebrate. You?

28. G3: How do you say *ambassadors* to another country?

29. I: Ambassadors. Ambassadors. But you know what happens a lot? Ambassadors from the United States are not bilingual. They are not bilingual. But it is preferable that they be bilingual. OK. Something else from your list. And here.

30. G2: No.

31. I: We have everything on your list? And here?

32. G1: They are immigra-immigrants.

33. I: Immigration can be associated with bilingualism. OK, let's look now at the concept of "bicultural," "bicultural." What do you have on your list? One thing you have on your list.

34. G6: Bilingual.

35. I: Bilingual. Someone who is bicultural also is bilingual. We will see because it is a theme we are going to discuss.

36. G5: *Europeans.*

37. I: Europeans are bicultural. OK.

38. G4: Students . . . *like* me . . . Americans . . . *Americans . . . but,* but . . . I have . . . how do you *background.*

39. I: Background, that you have a Latin or Hispanic background. Good. What do you have?

40. G3: Immigrants.

41. I: You also associate immigration with biculturalism? You, what do you have?

42. G2: Knowing many people other countries.

43. I: Knowing people from other countries. OK.

44. G1: Goes to church.

45. I: Bicultural and . . . going to church. Yes? And do you have something else that we have not mentioned?

46. G1: Living in two countries.

47. I: Living. Living. Having this intimate contact with another culture. What do you have on your list that we have not mentioned?

48. G6: Well educated.

49. I: Someone bicultural is also a well educated person. OK, good. Whichever group. Things that you have on your list that we have not mentioned.

50. G2: Traveling.

51. I: Travel a lot. Having experiences with other cultures. You.

52. G3: Television in the United States, food, the *Olympics.*

53. I: OK, the three things. The three things. Television, the Olympic Games, and food.
54. G2: Pers, perso, person from Sociology. The professor of Sociology.
55. I: Someone whose profession has to do with other cultures such as a professor of sociology. You, do you have something you want to add?
56. G3: How do you say *holidays*?
57. I: Holidays, festivals, the two. Holidays is probably the most common. Good. Yes, we also associate holidays with two cultures. OK, good.

Phase 2: Becoming bilingual/bicultural

58. I: Now we have all these concepts that we associate with bilingualism and with biculturalism. Now in Step 2, in Step 2, you have to think about how someone can become bilingual. More specifically, how can you, you yourselves, how can you become bilinguals? What do you have to do in the future to become bilingual? I want you to prepare a list of what, four things.
59. S1: I do not understand **llegar**. [Spanish expression **llegar a ser** for *to become*.]
60. I: In the future. You are going to be bilingual. How do you become bilingual? OK, in the future. You have some 3 minutes to do it.

    [*Monitors groups, provides lexical support.*]

    [*2 minutes later.*] Good, it seems that the great majority has finished. OK, let's see what ideas you propose. What ideas you propose for becoming bilingual. OK. I want to begin this time with you. What are two of the ideas you have? Two ideas.
61. G6: Study Spanish and travel to a Spanish-speaking country.
62. I: Study and travel. And do you have two different ideas that you can add to the list?
63. G5: Yes. Travel to other countries and take many, many language classes.
64. I: Basically they are the other group's ideas. You, what do you have?
65. G4: Attend all Spanish classes.
66. I: This is a good idea in general, in general. Yes, I agree with the idea. Another idea?
67. G4: Visit other country.
68. I: Good, three votes for visiting abroad. What ideas do you have?
69. G3: Practice the language a lot with your friends.
70. I: Yes, yes. If you have Spanish-speaking friends, well yes. It is a good way. Practice speech. Good. Another idea?
71. G3: [*Inaudible.*]
72. I: No? OK. Let's see, this group. What do you have?
73. G2: Speak with a lot of frequent the language.
74. I: OK, speak the language frequently. What else do you have?

75. G2: You can work with someone who speaks other languages.

76. I: Yes. Work with bilingual or monolingual people. What do you have?

77. G1: Watch television programs about other groups.

78. I: Uh hmm. Uh hmm. That is a good opportunity to develop your ear. Unfortunately in Champaign we do not have Univisión but in Chicago, yes. In Chicago, yes, there are Spanish channels. What else can you do? What other opportunities do you have to practice?

79. G1: Marry a bilingual person.

80. I: Get married to a bilingual person, OK. Or have a bilingual boy-friend or girlfriend. Have bilingual friends. What else? [*8-second pause.*] OK, anything else? Does someone want to add to the list? OK, good. Now you have 3 minutes to do Step 3. Step 3 has to do with biculturalism. How can you become bicultural?

[*Monitors groups, provides lexical support.*]

[*1 minute later.*] Good, you finished Step 3 quickly. I want to begin with you. Two ideas that you have for becoming bicultural.

81. G5: Read about.

82. I: Read about the culture. Very good. Another thing.

83. G5: Take Sociology classes about other countries.

84. I: OK, take classes on culture such as Sociology. You? What do you have?

85. G4: Another group I think.

86. I: OK. What do you have here? In the center.

87. G3: Celebrate more parties.

88. I: Celebrate more parties. Participate in parties. Yes, anything else?

89. G3: Live in other countries.

90. I: Yes, live in other countries. What do you have?

91. G2: Listen to *CDs*.

92. I: Yes, listen to music. Music is a cultural representation. What do you have?

93. G1: Be exchanges student.

94. I: Ah, very good. Study abroad as an exchange student. And now do you have anything?

95. G4: [*Inaudible*] change something [*inaudible*].

96. I: Again, please.

97. G4: No change something for differences.

98. I: Not change? or walk? [**Cambiar** versus **caminar** in Spanish.]

99. G4: Change.

100. I: Not change. Ah hah. Ah hah. Ah hah. I understand now. Good. OK.

Phase 3: Conclusion

101. I: I have a question for you. In your opinion, in your opinion, is it possible to be bilingual without being bicultural? Yes or no? How many say yes? Is it possible to be bilingual without being bicultural? How many say yes? [*Show of hands.*] Why? What are some reasons you can offer me? Yes?

102. s1: Only take classes about other languages in school.

103. I: If the only contact one has with the language is school contact. That's it. Another reason. [*4-second pause.*] Is it possible to be bicultural without being bilingual? Yes? For example, how? [*9-second pause.*]

104. s2: To learn about *Greece.*

105. I: Greece.

106. s2: I do not speak *Greece, Greek.*

107. I: Greek. Then what you are telling me is that there is a difference between bilingual and bicultural. It is that they are two different concepts. Other comments? Good.

6. Even though the main discourse routine of the learners was to create lists of associations and to propose ideas, they also had to present those associations and ideas to the instructor. Examine the transcripts for the discussions and the activities and find examples where the instructor negotiated meaning with the language learners as the result of a breakdown in communication.

7. The class discussion and the task-based activity presented in this research were mediated by an instructor figure. Examine the following transcripts of two groups of third-semester learners. One group was given discussion questions: What do you associate with bilingualism? What do you associate with biculturalism? The other group was given tasks as follows.

Step 1. As a group, prepare a list of everything you associate with the words *bilingual* and *bicultural.*

BILINGUAL	BICULTURAL
1. _____	1. _____
2. _____	2. _____
3. _____	3. _____
4. _____	4. _____
5. _____	5. _____

Analyze the transcript to see how much information comes out across the two formats and how meaning is negotiated.

Discussion Questions

Phase 1: Associations

1. s1: What do you associate with the word *bilingual*? Person that speaks two languages.

2. s2: Yes, and, ah, he speaks two languages good, ah, fluently.

3. s1: Fluently or not fluently?

4. s2: Fluently.

5. s1: More or less.

6. s2: Oh, more or less. What do you associate with the word *bicultural*?

7. s1: A person who knows two cultures, for example, Spanish, *Spanish,* and *Asian,* yes.

8. s2: And religious, religious, and, ah, possibly, ah, languages.

9. s1: Or a language.

10. s2: It is different in each country. It is part of the culture, I think.

Task-Based Activity

Phase 1: Associations

1. s4: Hello. Ah, Step 1. Ah. We prepare a list of everything that you associate with the words, ah, first, "bilingual."
2. s5: And bicultural.
3. s4: Ah. What is bilingual? Words and phrases.
4. s5: We are from different countries. And it is for . . .
5. s6: Ah, and, ah, people, ah, who speak two languages.
6. s5: Two or more.
7. s4: Ah, bilingual, ah, is not United State?
8. s5: Is what?
9. s4: *OK, most Americans aren't bilingual.*
10. s5: The schools, ah, I don't know. For, for bicultural, some people is from Colombia and five, six years the future, live in California, is bicultural.
11. s4: Immigration?
12. s5: Yes.
13. s4: And, ah, to visit. To visit? Yes, to visit another country. Can I, ah, be bicultural?
14. s5: Yes.
15. s6: Yes, ah, to be bicultural, a person needs, ah, he has, ah, a respect for the people, and the culture.
16. s5: And when a, ah, country, ah, *conquer*, another country, the countries are, ah, they are not, but, bicultural.
17. s4: Ah, war.
18. s5: War?
19. s4: *War.*
20. s5: Ah, thanks.
21. s5: Is this all for Step 1? Or one more? Huh?

CHAPTER 5

Implementing Interaction in the Classroom

CHAPTER OVERVIEW

No matter the subject matter, course content, teaching philosophy, or textbook, all instructors are responsible for implementing, maneuvering, and executing an instructional agenda. The ideas and issues presented in the previous chapters center on shifting the instructional agenda away from what Brooks (1992) termed the ping-pong game of question-answer sequences toward the redistribution of teaching and learning functions afforded by task-based instruction. In this chapter we examine task-based instruction in terms of three points of encounter: framing or introducing an activity, executing the steps of an activity with an eye toward the time constraints under which instructors operate, and concluding an activity. The examination begins with an analysis of the task-based interaction presented in Chapter 4 and then moves to suggestions for implementing the two activities developed in Chapter 3.

ROLES AND RESPONSIBILITIES

The instructional agenda is to shift the *communication = question & answer* paradigm toward *communication = expression, interpretation,* and *negotiation of meaning*. In this respect, Breen and Candlin (1979) have identified some essential components of the instructor/learner relationship.

> "Within a communicative methodology the teacher has two main roles. The first role is to facilitate the communicative process between *all* participants in the classroom, and between these participants and the various activities and texts. The second role is to act as *interdependent* participant within the learning-teaching group. . . . These roles imply a set of secondary roles for the teacher: first as an organizer of resources and as a resource himself. Second, as a guide within the classroom procedures and activities. . . . In guiding and monitoring the teacher needs to be a 'seer of potential' with the aim of facilitating and shaping individual and group knowledge and exploitation of abilities during learning" (p. 1; emphasis added).

71

Previous research has established that one instructor role/responsibility in the classroom is to impose social and linguistic parameters. These parameters can also be thought of as behavioral rules (Brooks 1992). Learning these behavioral rules has been referred to as developing classroom communicative competence (Wilkinson 1982, cited in Johnson 1995). In other words, instructors establish, monitor, and maintain acceptable ways for learners to participate in classroom lessons and activities. Language instructors typically exercise this authority by deciding the following (adapted from Allwright & Bailey 1991, p. 19; Brooks 1992; Johnson 1995, p. 4).

On a continuum with teacher-centered at one end and learner-centered at the other, interdependence is the middle point. It represents a balance. It is the counterpoint to the Atlas Complex described in Application Activity 2 in Chapter 2. It is what the instructors whose lessons were analyzed in Chapter 2 did not attain.

who can talk to whom	(turn taking)
about what	(topic initiation and topic shift)
in what ways	(tasks, interactional patterns)
for how long	(topic development, direction)
in what language	(code)
in what atmosphere	(tone)

In this chapter, we propose ways in which instructors can carry out the roles Breen and Candlin suggest by acting out the areas of authority Brooks, Allwright, and Bailey identify.

FACILITATING THE COMMUNICATION PROCESS AMONG ALL PARTICIPANTS

Let's examine how the instructor managed the task-based activity presented in Chapter 4. Tasks, interactional patterns, topic development, and direction were all decided a priori by creating the various steps that made up the activity. Overall the activity had three phases: associations with bilingualism and biculturalism; ways to become bilingual and bicultural; and the concluding discussion of the relationship between the two concepts. We focus in this section on the decisions the instructor made about turn taking, topic initiation, and topic shift.

The class was divided into six groups of three or four and assigned to complete Step 1. Each group made lists of its associations with the terms bilingual and bicultural. To manage the group interaction, the instructor announced a time limit and adhered to it rather strictly. At the end of the 3 minutes, each group reported to the class. The instructor asked for only one association with bilingualism. He extracted one item from each of the six groups and then went in reverse order, extracting another item from the six groups.

1. I: I have here a worksheet to distribute. Good. First, I want you to divide into groups of four, groups of four people. Here we have four, and four. Divide yourselves into four people. [*5-second pause.*] Instead of having a group of five, we can have three here. OK. As a group, as a group I want you to do Step 1. OK. You have to prepare two lists. Three minutes. You have three minutes to do Step 1.

[*Groups work for 3 minutes. Instructor monitors groups, answers questions, supplies lexical items.*]

[*After 2 minutes.*] You have one more minute.

[*1 minute later.*] OK, let's see. Let's see what things you associate first with bilingual, with this term. What do you associate with the term bilingual? OK. You, one thing, one thing that you have on your list.

2. G1: Difficult.

3. I: Difficult. It is difficult to be bilingual. OK. And you, one thing.

4. G2: Speak more than one language.

Finally, the instructor opened the floor to any group that had an association that had not yet been mentioned; ten more associations emerged. This request for volunteers is the only one in the entire session.

29. I: OK. Whatever group has something on their list that has not already been mentioned. Do you have something, something that we have not mentioned up til now?

In exercising his authority to assign turn taking, the instructor maximized the distribution of participation among as many groups and learners as possible. By way of contrast, had he allowed the first group to name all five of its associations, he would have run the risk of other groups not having anything new to contribute to the growing information base.

When calling for the class's associations with the term "bicultural," he started with Group 4 rather than 1 or 6, thereby breaking up the clockwise/counterclockwise flow of information. Again, he asked groups to name only one item. After allowing each group to give an item, he moved to the next step of the activity. He did not open up the floor because he felt time was beginning to get away from him. Since the first follow-up had taken more time than anticipated, he decided to exercise his authority to cease topic development and to shift topics. He announced a 3-minute time limit on the next step, that is, proposing ideas on how to become bilingual. When groups finished, he asked each one to state two (rather than just one) of its ideas. The motivation to require two ideas originated in the amount of time it took to have each group present one idea. He started with Group 6 and then moved to Group 1.

He then assigned the groups to complete Step 3, proposing ideas on how to become bicultural, and gave them 3 minutes to do it even though they finished in half the time. When he asked the groups to report, he did so moving from Group 1 to Group 6, reversing the order of the previous round. Once again, each group gave two ideas. The instructor firmly controlled the turn taking; he selected which group would speak and how much it would speak. The result of such control was to evenly distribute the participation.

To conclude the activity, the instructor posed questions about the relationship between being bicultural and bilingual. He did two things to encourage participation. First, before asking the questions he told the class they had to offer him their opinions. By doing so, he announced to them that he was not asking rhetorical questions but questions that required their response.

97. I: Now I have some questions for you. OK? Questions. You have to offer me some opinions, some opinions, OK? Is it possible, is it possible to be bilingual without being bicultural?

Then he had the class identify its overall opinion by a show of hands. This allowed him to identify potential participants had there been no volunteers. In this case there was a volunteer who perhaps felt encouraged to participate since he had already committed himself to an opinion by raising his hand.

98. SS: Yes.
99. I: You say yes?
100. S1: Maybe.
101. I: Maybe? You say yes. How many of you say yes? There were many people. [Show of hands.] What are some of your reasons? Who can offer me reasons? Why can you be bilingual without being bicultural? Sir.

IMPLEMENTING THE INSTRUCTIONAL EVENT

In the following discussion the term *instructional event* is used to refer both to a single activity viewed in its entirety and to an entire lesson comprised of a sequence of activities. To manage any instructional event, instructors should frame the event by indicating its purpose, place in the sequence of activities, and/or the expected outcome for the students. Instructors must be aware of and exert control over time: Time constrains all instruction. To manage an instructional event that has multiple components, be they steps in a single activity or a sequence of activities, instructors must be concerned with executing each aspect of the activity. Finally, instructors should conclude the activity. If there is a desired outcome, instructors should signal that the outcome has been achieved. These four constructs (framing, time constraints, executing, and concluding) will focus the discussion of implementing the instructional event encapsulated in the task-based activities presented in Chapter 2. We agree with Ur (1996) in that "the success of group work depends to some extent on the surrounding social climate, and on how habituated the class is to using it; and also, of course, on the selection of an interesting and stimulating task whose performance is well within the ability of the group. But it also depends, more immediately, on *effective and careful organization*" (pp. 232–233; emphasis added).

In this chapter we offer concrete examples and suggestions for implementing the interaction generated by task-based activities. Doing so will be a process that Legutke and Thomas describe as follows.

"... [T]he central methodological challenge, for both teacher and student, consists of creating the learning space (Stevick 1980) within which interaction is to unfold. To mobilize the interactive potential of the classroom learning situation, they do not only need to be aware of its dimensions, they need to be able to set up points of encounter for the components and participants in the interaction. ... Only through such encounters is a process of balancing out, of negotiating together, and of learning set in motion" (1991, p. 15).

The instructional event is an encounter of people, methods, and materials, and it is left to the instructor to implement this event.

THREE POINTS OF ENCOUNTER

Framing

Every instructor introduces an activity, exercise, or practice. Some are utilitarian and business-like. For example, "Open your books to page 130. Let's do Activity A." When an introduction focuses on the content, communicative purpose, or outcome of an activity, we say that it frames the activity. For example, "We can think of the things we do as physically active or not. If they are not, they are sedentary. Are we physically active or are we physically sedentary? Open your books to page 130. Let's do Activity A and we will find out."

Execution and Time Constraints

Moving learners through the various steps of an activity is an essential element in implementing the instructional event because language learning takes place via the completion of the various tasks involved. "The lesson is a type of organized social event that occurs in virtually all cultures. Lessons in different places may vary in topic, time, place, atmosphere, methodology, and materials, but they all, essentially, are concerned with learning as their main objective, involve the participation of learner(s) and teachers, and are limited and pre-scheduled as regards time, place, and membership" (Ur 1996, p. 213). In this section of the chapter, we address the limited and pre-scheduled nature of lessons. All lessons take place in real time, and time, consequently, must be used by the instructor; the instructor cannot fall victim to time.

We have chosen to link the concepts of executing and time constraints because announcing the time learners have to carry out a step is the final statement an instructor needs to make about executing a step. Moreover, the time announced, be it 2 minutes or 10, should be strictly adhered to. When it comes to time limits, the instructor's behavior establishes a social parameter for the learners; they will behave according to the instructor's behavior. During the task-based activity presented in Chapter 4, the instructor announced a 3-minute time limit for Steps 1 and 2 and strictly adhered to them. By Step 3, the learners were familiar with the task and the time limit such that they completed this step in 2 minutes. If an instructor announces a 2-minute limit and then regularly does not call time for 10 minutes, he or she is not efficiently or effectively maneuvering the instructional event. The learners quickly infer that the instructor is not serious about time limits, which means that they leisurely can work through any or all steps of the activity. Another approach to time limits appears more flexible but serves equally well to send the message to learners about completing their work. An instructor can announce a time limit minus a minute or two. Then, as the instructor monitors group work, he or she can announce another minute or two for the learners to complete their work. In both approaches the instructor exerts control over how much time learners spend on their tasks.

Concluding

When we hold discussions, we naturally make an attempt to bring them to a conclusion. If two people are comparing their families, one possible conclusion of the discussion would be that Family A is not as dysfunctional as Family B. Or, if two people are discussing a mistake or error in judgment that one of them made, each of the following statements could conclude the interaction. Each has a different effect.

  a. Well, don't worry about it.
  b. I know it won't happen again.
  c. The past is the past and we don't want to see it repeated.

On the topic of study habits, two people might conclude that they put in equal time and effort.

  a. You're as much of a workaholic as I am.
  b. You stress as much as I do.
  c. We're peas in a pod.

In that task-based activities are alternative structures for classroom discussions, they, too, should be brought to a conclusion. Suggestions for concluding each of the activities presented in Chapter 3 follow. You should note that the conclusion tends to tie back into the frame, which helps reinforce the purposefulness of the various steps in the interaction. An instructional event comprised of three activities also could be visually represented as follows, if the conclusion of each activity referred back to its frame.

Let's now apply these three concepts to Activities A.1 What Did You Do Last Week? and B.1 The Best Shows on TV.

Moving linearly from A to B to C	↓	Activity A		Tying the conclusion back to the frame
	↓	Activity B		
	↓	Activity C		

Framing

To frame Activity A.1, an instructor can begin by referring to the outcome of the activity. In this case, the outcome is a profile of the class's week as sedentary or active. The instructor can begin the instructional event by writing the phrase "last week" on the board, explaining that during the activity the class will be discussing what they did last week and that they will have to evaluate what they did as sedentary, active, or just as sedentary as active.

I: In this activity we will talk about what we did last week. We will find out if last week was sedentary, active, or something in between. Just as sedentary as active.

As the instructor uses each of these words, he or she can write them on the board or reveal them on a prepared overhead to yield the following visual display.

```
┌──────────────────────────────────────────────────────────┐
│                                                            │
│                       LAST WEEK                            │
│                                                            │
│         sedentary     as sedentary     active             │
│                         as active                          │
│                                                            │
└──────────────────────────────────────────────────────────┘
```

This display can be left on the board or overhead throughout the activity since it can be used as the basis for executing Steps 4 and 5 (presented below).

Execution and Time Constraints

In Activity A.1, the tasks include class agreement on categorizing activities, comparing lists of activities, and drawing a class profile. Each of these tasks can be executed in a variety of ways. Step 1 requires the instructor to announce that the interactional pattern is partners and that the time limit is 2 minutes.

I: Work in pairs on Step 1 for 2 minutes. Evaluate each activity. You have 2 minutes. Begin.

The step finishes with an assessment of the categorizations because, in order for the class to draw a profile of their activities, they must all agree on the criteria for assessing the nature of an activity. This task is important to the final outcome of the activity, but it clearly should be carried out as quickly as possible because it is not the heart of the interaction. The most expedient means for determining agreement is for the instructor to call for a show of hands. For each activity, the instructor determines by show of hands how many people indicated an activity was sedentary or active. Any differences of opinion should be resolved either by how the majority votes or by instructor prerogative.

i: Let's see if you agree on the evaluations. How many of you say dancing at a party is sedentary? How many of you say it is active? Complete agreement. Dancing is active. What about riding a bike? How many say it is sedentary? How many say it is active?

To move to Step 2, the instructor can tell the class to continue working with the same partner and that they have another 2 minutes to complete Step 2.

i: Now do Step 2. You can probably do it in 2 minutes. Begin.

The instructor is then faced with another task to implement, that of comparing lists. The decision regarding how to execute this task depends on the function of the list in the activity. Clearly Step 1 provides linguistic support to the learners. The relationship between Steps 1 and 2 is that Step 2 allows learners to add to the list of considerations activities that they themselves have actually engaged in, thereby giving a personal dimension to the activity. The relationship between Steps 2 and 3 is that the lists make the interview easier to carry out because they provide the learners a quick and easy reference to the content of the interview. In other words, Step 2 allows learners the opportunity to add personalized activities to the list while the lists function as linguistic support for the interviews. The best decision regarding the execution of Step 2, then, is based on looking ahead to Step 3, the interview. The instructor can, therefore, ask several pairs of learners for their list of three activities and write them on the board and then ask the rest of the class to add any item to the list that has not already been mentioned. Of course, it is not necessary that the instructor be the one to write on the board; a class member can do so just as well. (This option applies only to languages in which the orthographic system is not an issue in the learning of the second language.)

i: Carlos, would you write things on the board? Thanks. Here's a piece of chalk. Now, go ahead up there. Now, let's find out what you have added. This group, here. What are your three activities? [*Group responds. Volunteer writes on the board.*] Fine. This group over here. What are your three activities? [*Group responds. Volunteer writes on the board.*] From anyone in any group. Do you have something to add that has not yet been mentioned?

The instructor should then direct the learners to carry out Step 3. The interview is the heart of the interaction between learners; this step requires them to use the second language to learn and gather information from each other. The time limit should, therefore, reflect the importance of this phase of the activity. Setting a time limit of about 10 minutes should allow sufficient time for each participant to ask and then answer questions.

i: Go ahead and do Step 3 now. You have to interview each other using the activities we came up with in the previous steps. You have ten minutes.

To be sure that each learner has the opportunity to interview the other one, the instructor should monitor the time, announcing at the end of 5 minutes that if one person hasn't been interviewed the pairs should switch roles. At the end of 8 minutes, the instructor should announce that 2 minutes remain. Finally, at the end of 10 minutes, the announced time limit, he or she should direct the partners to carry out Step 4, their evaluations of each other. These evaluations will require less than 30 seconds.

I: Five minutes more. You should start the second interview now. [*3 minutes later.*] Two more minutes. [*2 minutes later.*] All right. Use what you learned in Step 3 and do Step 4 now. Do it quickly.

While the class is carrying out Steps 3 and 4, the instructor should go to the board and create the rating scale out of the visual used to frame Activity A.1. He or she can do so by adding the numbers of the rating scale and the word *very* to the visual. This move helps tie the frame to the conclusion.

LAST WEEK

very sedentary		as sedentary as active		very active
1	2	3	4	5

The task in Step 5 is to use the evaluations to draw a profile of the class as having spent an active or sedentary week. The profile task, in this case, requires that a generalization be drawn from specific examples. To do so, the instructor should direct the class to answer for their partners (thereby making the pairs responsible for the group work) and should pose questions in terms of the partner. The instructor can count the number of hands raised and write the number under the appropriate number on the scale. This procedure can be repeated for each number on the scale. Alternatively, a class member can do the tallying on the board.

I: Carlos, would you write on the board again? OK. I want you to answer for your partner. Tell me about your partner. Show of hands. How many put number 1, very sedentary, for their partner? [*Counts hands.*] Carlos, put a 1. How many chose number 2, sedentary, for their partners? [*Counts hands.*] Carlos, put a 7. How many thought that last week was just as sedentary as active for their partner? [*Counts hands.*] Carlos, put a 4. . . .

Concluding

The final step of Activity A.1 makes coming to a conclusion fairly easy since the instructor and class have concrete information on the board. The instructor can end the activity by making a concluding statement such as the following.

I: Looking at the numbers on the scale, I believe that we have a wide variety of people in the class. Some people are very active, some are not. But overall, I think there is a balance.

The alternative is to attempt to involve each learner in deriving a conclusion. Underneath the tally marks, the instructor could write the phrase "In conclusion . . ." and direct each class member to complete the phrase.

I: I want each of you to look at the numbers on the scale and then finish the sentence that begins, In conclusion. . . . Write your answers as quickly as possible. One minute.

LAST WEEK

very sedentary		as sedentary as active		very active
1	2	3	4	5
1	7	4	10	3

In conclusion . . .

Involving each person in the conclusion is a technique that helps evenly distribute the participation pattern. After a minute, the instructor can ask for a volunteer to read his or her conclusion, and then ask several more to do so. If different conclusions are being reached, the instructor can ask for a show of hands to see the degree of agreement with the different conclusions. If the volunteers are expressing consensus, the instructor can ask for a show of hands to determine if such consensus is widespread. The option an instructor selects depends on how a particular group of learners responds. The selected option can change from one class hour to the next.

ACTIVITY B.1   THE BEST SHOWS ON TV

Framing

To frame Activity B.1, an instructor can present the following visual to the class and tell them the following.

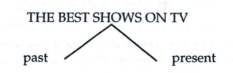

ɪ: Watching TV is something that I am sure most of you do. Today we will talk about the best shows on TV. Shows that are on now as well as shows that used to be on. For this activity, we will say that reruns are shows from the past even though they are still on today.

An alternative is simply to write the word *TV* on the board and ask the class how many watch TV 5 days/nights per week.

ɪ: How many of you watch TV at least five days or nights a week? [*Show of hands.*] Well, I am glad that so many of you watch TV because you should have something to say about the best shows on TV, which is what the next activity talks about. We will talk about the best shows on TV both from the past and the present.

A note of caution is called for on using personalized questions as a standard means of framing an activity. It is not advisable for instructors to ask learners the specific questions that the learners are supposed to ask each other during the activity. The question the instructor poses to frame Activity B.1 is not a question the learners will ask each other. Likewise, the instructor relates his own activities as the alternative frame for Activity A.1. He does not ask learners what they did because that is precisely the question they will pose to each other.

Execution and Time Constraints

Step 1 entails dividing the class into seven groups and assigning to each group one of the items that make up Step 1.

ɪ: Complete the assigned sentence with three pieces of information. You have 5 minutes.

Presenting the results of the group work and being responsible for the products of group interaction is built into Step 2. The instructor has options for orchestrating this presentation. The direction lines indicate that learners note what other groups present because they will need that information in Step 3. How does an instructor ensure that learners take note? The instructor who taught Lesson 1 in Chapter 2 assumed responsibility when she asked a series of questions after each group's presentation. She could have decided to write each group's description of its unique person on the board. That decision also would have removed from the learners themselves the responsibility for comprehending and gathering information. They are the ones who need the information; they should take note of it from each other. What can we do to ensure that learners report to each other and not only to the instructor?

ɪ: For Step 2, each group presents its information. The rest of you, all of you, must take notes. You must write down what others say. You need this for Step 3. Let's begin

Classrooms that have furniture define and delimit learner space from instructor space. The desk in the front of the room provides not only a physical boundary between instructor and learners, but a mental one as well. Instructors may wander into learner space, but learners must be invited to wander into instructor space. For example, many instructors consider the board "their space" or their domain. They don't even think of ways to bring learners into that sphere.

with A. What do you have? [*Group reports.*] Do the rest of you agree? Does anyone want to add to this? Elaine, do you want to add to the list? [*Students respond.*] All right. Let's see, Jennifer. Would you read the entire list of items we now have for A? [*Jennifer responds.*] You didn't write them down? You need to. Who can read the entire list?

Step 3 requires the class to provide examples of TV shows that fit their categories. One option for carrying out this task is for the instructor to write each category on the board—Women, Men, Children, etc.—such that each category is a column heading.

I: Brent, would you write the names of TV shows on the board as people suggest them? Thanks. How about Group A? What is one of the best shows in terms of how women are presented? [*Group responds.*] How does this show fit our descriptions? [*Group responds.*] Group B, what show can you come up with for the presentation of women? [*Group responds.*] How does it fit our descriptions?

On the one hand, the suggested management of this step has the instructor determining who takes the next turn, which is certainly an instructor prerogative. The point in doing so is not so much to exert Atlas-like control over the interaction, but rather to distribute participation as evenly as possible across all class members.

Concluding

The execution of the final step of Activity B.1 yields lists of shows in each category. To tie the activity's conclusion back into the frame, the instructor can ask the class to count the number of shows listed that were on in the past and the number that are on presently. He can write those numbers under the visual he used to frame the activity and make a concluding, summarizing statement such as, "It seems that the past offers more of the best shows on TV than the present does!"

I: Now that we have shows in each of the categories, I want this half of the class to count up how many shows are from the past. I want the other half of the class to count the number of shows from the present. Go ahead and do that now. [*Pause.*] How many of these shows are from the past? [*Instructor writes the number under the word "past" in the visual used to frame the activity.*] How many of these shows are from the present? [*Instructor writes the number under the word "present" in the visual used to frame the activity.*] Now, I have one more question to ask you. Are TV shows better today than they were in the past?

SUMMARY

"We do not manage interaction purely for its own sake. We manage interaction in the language classroom for the sake of giving everyone the best possible opportunities for learning the language. . . . In this way, managing interaction and managing learning come together" (Allwright & Bailey 1991, p. 21). Allwright and Bailey certainly capture the underlying purpose of this chapter. Implementing interaction in the classroom is the primary way in which instructors make maximum use of their resources. These resources consist of both the materials or activities and the participants in the activities. The decisions and techniques used to manage the activity analyzed in Chapter 3 provided concrete examples of ways instructors control turn taking, topic initiation, topic shift, topic development, and direction. These techniques were then employed to hypothesize different ways of carrying out the two task-based activities developed in Chapter 2. Moreover, the tripartite framework of framing, executing, and concluding was used to demonstrate these techniques for implementing interactions.

GAINING GREATER PERSPECTIVE

1. *Planning Lessons.* Lee (1989) and Shrum and Glisan (1994) offer chapters on lesson planning. Lee emphasizes the individual differences across instructors while noting that lesson plans primarily organize time and material. Shrum and Glisan offer suggestions for planning at several layers of the instructional process: curricular, unit, and daily plans. Ballman (1996) demonstrates a week's worth of lesson planning. Her article may be particularly helpful in that the communicative activities she uses as examples are generated from a task-based framework. Nunan (1989, Chapter 6) provides a framework for sequencing task-based activities inside a daily lesson, which he terms *task continuity:* "chaining of activities together to form a sequence, for which the successful completion of prior activities is a prerequisite for succeeding ones" (p. 119). Legutke and Thomas (1991, Chapter 5) move task-based instruction from the small-scale activity to what they term "learning in projects" (p. 158).

2. *Managing Interaction.* Ur (1996, p. 234) provides guidelines for organizing group work that, in many respects, parallel the concepts presented in this chapter. She also provides lists of practical suggestions regarding lesson preparation (pp. 215–222).

3. *Roles.* Brown and Palmer (1988, pp. 37–38) provide a pedagogically oriented list of learner roles in communicative activities: actors, assistants, doers, initiators, judges, learners, observers, patients, players, props, providers, recorders, sources of information, teachers, workers. Many of these context-defined roles can be found in Activities A.1 and B.1. Interestingly, selecting student roles is one of the seven strategies Brown and Palmer recommend for developing ideas into teaching activities, indicating the fundamental importance of the learners' role in communicative language teaching. Nunan (1989, Chapter 4) provides a summary of roles for learners and instructors categorized by language teaching method. His work is largely based on Richards and Rogers' (1986) analysis of methods, a book worth reading in its own right.

4. *Building on Each Other.* Nunan (1989) suggests that tasks be sequenced so that the outcome of one is necessary for carrying out the next task. Coleman (1987) also makes a similar suggestion. What they term *separate activities that build on each other* can be found in this book, which uses a step-by-step

approach to carrying out task-based activities. These steps would represent several small activities for Nunan and Coleman. Nunan does not provide examples of these activities; Coleman, on the other hand, provides an excellent example (pp. 132–142).

APPLICATION ACTIVITIES

1. Now that you have scripts for each of the activities, try to have yourself videotaped teaching one or more of them. Compare your planned execution to what really took place in class. How similar are they? How different? What brought about the differences?
2. Give one of the activities to an experienced instructor and ask him or her to talk about how he or she would execute it. Record the discussion. Do the same thing with an inexperienced instructor. Then analyze the different decisions each makes regarding orchestration of the activity. What decisions are similar to or different from the ones presented in this chapter? Do they both refer to framing, executing, time constraints, and concluding?
3. Script how you would implement the interaction for the following activity (adapted from Lee, Binkowski, & VanPatten 1994, p. 116). Imagine that you are addressing a group of second-semester learners. For the sake of this exercise, assume that vocabulary is not an issue.

Activity. How Do You React?

Step 1. What do you think about the idea of eating or drinking the following foods? Use the scale to indicate your reaction.

Yes, I would like to try it.		Yes, but only a little.		Only if it were absolutely necessary.
1	2	3	4	5

1. _____ a glass of camel's milk
2. _____ a cup of coffee with camel's milk
3. _____ meat preserved via radiation treatment
4. _____ meat preserved via radiation treatment after it was stored for 8 years
5. _____ seaweed salad
6. _____ seaweed soup
7. _____ fruit preserved via radiation treatment
8. _____ fruit heavily treated with pesticides
9. _____ monkey brains
10. _____ roe (fish eggs: caviar)

Step 2. Compare your reactions to those of one or two classmates. Do you agree on your preferences?

Step 3. Compare your reactions to those of the rest of the class. What foods does the majority want to try? What foods would the majority try only if it were absolutely necessary?

Step 4. Which statement best describes the class?
   a. Eating is an adventure and we are adventurers.

b. We are somewhat conservative in our tastes.

c. We would eat anything if we had to.

d. We would rather die than try certain foods.

e. Other: _____

4. Consider an alternative frame for Activity A.1   What Did You Do Last Week? Many instructors like to personalize activities as a means to (a) model the activity, and (b) establish an affectively positive class environment. An instructor could begin by telling the class what he or she did last week after writing the phrase "last week" on the board, and then evaluate those activities as sedentary or active. To transition from personal information into the activity, the instructor could tell the class that for this activity, they will be interviewing each other about what they did last week in order to profile the class as a whole to determine if last week was sedentary or active for them. Are there advantages to this personalized frame? How much time would it take to do this? Should time be a factor in considering alternatives? If this is the frame, what would the conclusion be?

5. Consider redesigning Step 3 of Activity B.1   The Best Shows on TV. As formulated, Step 3 has the whole class offering examples of TV shows. This step could, however, be reformulated toward group interaction. How could groups come up with examples of TV shows while at the same time not be engaged in gratuitous group work? How do you bring the entire activity to a conclusion?

CHAPTER 6

Tasks for Non-Beginners

CHAPTER OVERVIEW

The activities developed in Chapter 3 were designed for beginning language learners. A natural question to explore now is, How can task-based interaction be developed for non-beginning language learners? In this chapter we present principles for developing task-based activities for non-beginners. Those principles are then applied to the two activities originally developed in Chapter 3. Finally, suggestions are offered for implementing one of the activities designed for non-beginners, focusing once again on the three points of encounter explored in Chapter 5.

CRITERIA FOR DEVELOPING ACTIVITIES FOR NON-BEGINNING LANGUAGE LEARNERS

Previous work in the area of curricular sequencing approaches the question of level-appropriate language learning activities in different ways. VanPatten (1987) derived suggestions for curricular sequencing (beginning, intermediate, advanced learners) based on a developing concept of the roles of input and output in second language development. Omaggio Hadley (1986, 1993) utilizes the ACTFL Proficiency Guidelines, which she refers to as "descriptions of typical competencies (as well as patterns of weakness) of language users in each of the ranges of proficiency" (1986, p. 176), as the basis for curricular planning in teaching language skills (reading, listening, speaking, writing). For example, in the area of speaking, the Guidelines refer to functions such as expressing minimal courtesy and agreement/disagreement at the Novice level; to get into, through, and out of a simple survival situation at the Intermediate level; and, at the Advanced level, to talk one's way out of trouble. Nunan (1991, pp. 113–115) also bases his recommendations for grading tasks according to a set of specifications reminiscent of the ACTFL Proficiency Guidelines. His informational specifications include comprehending and carrying out simple instructions for physical actions for Beginners; listening to a sequence of instructions and transforming the information by completing a table, map, or diagram for Pre-Intermediate learners; and giving a set of aural and written instructions on how to make or assemble something for Intermediates.

A very different approach to curricular sequencing, one more relevant to the present discussion than the Guidelines or Nunan's specifications, is found in aspects of the work by Brindley (1987), Candlin (1987), and Prabhu (1987), all cited in Nunan. Brindley (p. 109 of Nunan 1991) approaches the question of curricular sequencing by addressing factors that make what the learner has to do more or less complex. Under task complexity, he poses the following questions.

- How many steps are in the question?
- How complex are the instructions?
- What cognitive demands does the task make on the learner?
- How much information is the learner expected to process in performing the task?
- Is the language that learners are expected to produce in line with their processing capacity?

Candlin (1987) echoes Brindley's concern for cognitive demands. He states

> ". . . we may be able to design tasks in which there is a gradual increase in cognitive complexity without dramatically raising the communicative load. For example, tasks which require learners to follow a clear chronological sequence, referring to individual actions of individual characters, will clearly be cognitively less demanding than a task in which there is no such clear development and where the picture is complicated by multiple actions and multiple actors" (p. 19).

Prabhu's concerns for task difficulty grew out of his experience in the Bangalore Project on communicative language teaching (see Beretta 1987 for a description of the Bangalore project). He maintains that difficulty is related to the amount and type of information handled, the number of steps or cognitive operations required, learners' knowledge of the world, and the abstractness of the concepts handled in the activity.

Given the preceding discussion of previous work on curricular sequencing and task difficulty, the following criteria are used to structure the activities for higher levels of instruction. In comparing the higher levels to the first-year level, we can do any or all of the following that result in making the activities more cognitively demanding.

If you were to propose a new textbook to a publisher, you would be asked about the scope and sequence. *Scope* refers to the grammar items included in the book. What grammar would you include? Would you exclude any particular grammar items usually found in textbooks? *Sequence* refers to the order of presentation of the selected grammar items. Is the sequence the same as that in other books? Are you proposing to alter the sequence? Curricular sequencing has long been associated with and driven by grammar-related concerns. Other concerns, such as how to structure interaction, have been of secondary if not tertiary importance to publishers and instructors alike.

a. Increase the information load.

b. Explore more subtopics or more complex subtopics.

c. Alter the linguistic support provided.

When moving to higher levels, it may not be necessary to change an activity along all three dimensions. Depending on the activity, it may not be necessary, for example, to increase information load and explore more complex subtopics as well as alter the way linguistic support is provided. It may be sufficient only to increase the information load. Likewise, it may be sufficient to explore more subtopics while altering the way linguistic support is provided. The criteria, in other words, should be applied in a flexible rather than rigid way.

In this chapter we will apply these three criteria to the two activities developed in Chapter 3. We begin with Activity A.1   What Did You Do Last Week? and from it develop Activity A.2   More Physically or More Mentally Active? and Activity A.3   Mentally and Physically Active. Suggestions are then offered for developing Activities B.2 and B.3   The Best and Worst of TV Shows. Activities A.2 and A.3 serve to illustrate the process by which an instructor can develop activities for higher-level language learners. They are not meant to suggest that all an instructor need do to create a coherent curriculum is recycle the same set of activities from level to level.

ACTIVITY A.2   MORE PHYSICALLY OR MORE MENTALLY ACTIVE?

Activity A.1   What Did You Do Last Week? required learners to categorize activities as physically sedentary or active. Then pairs of learners interviewed each other in order to rate how sedentary or active their partner's week was. Finally, they drew a class profile. (You may want to reread Activity A.1 in Chapter 3 and compare it to Activity A.2.) Activity A.2   More Physically or More Mentally Active? is more cognitively complex than Activity A.1 in that the information load has been increased and more subtopics have been incorporated. The way in which linguistic support is provided has not been altered. The increase in information load as well as the exploration of a more complex subtopic carry with them a greater cognitive demand. This increase in cognitive demand is evident in the fact that the dual perspective of physical versus mental activity is established in Step 1 and maintained through Step 5. The learners have more to think about, ponder, and take into consideration at every step along the way to completing the activity. As you read over Activity A.2   More Physically or More Mentally Active?, note how the concept of multiple perspectives has been incorporated into the activity structure.

Activity A.2   More Physically or More Mentally Active?

Step 1. Indicate if each activity is mentally or physically active.

	MENTALLY ACTIVE	PHYSICALLY ACTIVE
1. dancing at a party	❏	❏
2. riding a bike	❏	❏

3. playing video games ☐ ☐

4. playing a sport ☐ ☐

5. reading a book ☐ ☐

6. watching TV ☐ ☐

7. writing a letter ☐ ☐

8. making dinner ☐ ☐

Step 2. Working in groups of two or three, verify your answers. Then add up to six other activities to the list. Half should involve mental activity and the other half physical activity.

	MENTALLY ACTIVE	PHYSICALLY ACTIVE
9. _____	☐	☐
10. _____	☐	☐
11. _____	☐	☐
12. _____	☐	☐
13. _____	☐	☐
14. _____	☐	☐

Step 3. Share the results of Step 2 with the rest of the class. Are there any activities you want to add to your list?

Step 4. Interview a classmate to determine what he or she did last week. Be sure to keep track of the answers because you will need them in Step 5.

Step 5. Use the following scales to evaluate the type of week your partner had last week. Then determine if the class as a whole was more mentally or more physically active last week.

Mental Activity			Physical Activity		
Very	Somewhat	Not at All	Very	Somewhat	Not at All
1 2	3	4 5	1 2	3	4 5

Activity A.2   More Physically or More Mentally Active? requires learners to manipulate a greater information load than does Activity A.1. The second steps of Activities A.1 and A.2 are also different. The information load in Activity A.2 has been increased so that learners produce six activities (three physically active and three mentally active) to add to the list, compared to the three activities produced in Activity A.1.

One of the subtopics in both Activities A.1 and A.2 is to find out what classmates did last week. Requiring learners to account for the dual perspective of mental and physical activity in Activity A.2 not only increases the information load, but is a more complex approach to the subtopic. Activity A.1 explores the single subtopic of physical activity whereas Activity A.2 explores the subtopics of physical and mental activity. Imagine the interaction in the paired interview in Step 4. For Activity A.2, learners will have to gather information about both types of activities and will have to gather sufficient information on both types to make the dual evaluation called for in Step 5.

ACTIVITY A.3   MENTALLY AND PHYSICALLY ACTIVE

To create a third version of Activity A.1 suitable for an even higher level of language learner, we have increased the information load, explored a more complex subtopic, *and* altered the way in which linguistic support is provided. Activity A.3   Mentally and Physically Active requires learners to account for two perspectives on activities, mental and physical, which is also the dual perspective incorporated into Activity A.2   More Physically or More Mentally Active? One of the greatest differences between Activities A.1, A.2, and A.3 is that the first two require learners to be responsible for information they gather on only one other person. Activity A.3, on the other hand, requires learners to be responsible for information they generate in groups (Steps 1 and 4) and gather together from other groups' reports (Steps 2, 3, and 5). The paired interview that characterizes the heart of Activities A.1 and A.2 has been replaced in Activity A.3 by a group task, followed by a presentation of the group work in Step 5, and culminating in evaluating the information other groups present.

The following are among the differences between Activities A.1, A.2, and A.3 that contribute to Activity A.3 being more cognitively complex. First, physical/mental was presented as a binary option in Activities A.1 and A.2; the activities learners evaluated were either physically active or mentally active. Activity A.3 presents physical/mental not as a binary option but as more complex, interrelated phenomena. Second, at this higher level, learners must propose in Step 4 how a physical activity can be made more mental or a mental activity made more physical. Third, Activities A.1 and A.2 provided learners concrete rating scales with which to evaluate information, Activity A.3 has no rating scale for learners to use. They must take notes on other groups' reports. Finally, the conclusions reached across the three versions of the activity are very different. The end result of Activities A.1 and A.2 is to draw a class profile. The end result of Activity A.3 is more complex in that learners must reach a conclusion about the ease or difficulty of interrelating physical and mental activity. In other words, the conclusion to Activity A.3 requires more abstract thinking than the conclusions to Activities A.1 and A.2, based as they are on concrete rating scales.

All three versions of Activity A provide learners lexical support via the list of activities to categorize in Step 1. Activities A.1 and A.2 are no different from each other in terms of the way linguistic support is provided. Activity A.3, however, distinguishes itself from the other two. In Step 4, learners must complete if/then statements. (Although true for English and Romance languages, that particular structure might not be the appropriate one in all languages.) Learners have been moved from the lexical level to the sentence level. In the process, they needed to use particular grammatical structures.

Activity A.3   Mentally and Physically Active

Step 1. Working in groups, indicate if each activity is mentally or physically active.

	MENTALLY ACTIVE	PHYSICALLY ACTIVE
1. dancing at a party	❑	❑
2. riding a bike	❑	❑
3. playing video games	❑	❑
4. playing a sport	❑	❑
5. reading a book	❑	❑
6. watching TV	❑	❑
7. writing a letter	❑	❑
8. making dinner	❑	❑
9. _____	❑	❑

Step 2. First, present your ideas on activities that you classified as physically active in Step 1. Listen and note the ideas the other groups present.

Step 3. Now present your ideas on activities that you clarified as mentally active in Step 1. Listen and note the ideas the other groups present.

Step 4. Then, working in groups of three, complete the following sentences of each of the activities in Step 1.

1. If dancing at a party involved _____ , then it would also involve mental activity.
2. If riding a bike involved _____ , then it would also involve _____ activity.
3. If playing video games involved_____ , then it would also involve _____ activity.
4. If playing a sport involved _____ , then it would also involve _____ activity.
5. If reading a book involved _____ , then it would also involve _____ activity.
6. If watching TV involved _____ , then it would also involve _____ activity.
7. If writing a letter involved _____ , then it would also involve _____ activity.
8. If making dinner involved _____ , then it would also involve _____ activity.
9. If _____ involved _____ , then it would also involve _____ activity.

Step 5. Go over the results of Step 4 with the rest of the class. Then decide as a class which of the following statements is true.
   a. It is easier to add mental activity to a physical one.
   b. It is easier to add physical activity to a mental one.
   c. It is just as easy to add mental activity to a physical one as it is to add physical activity to a mental one.
   d. Other: _____

ACTIVITIES B.2 AND B.3   THE BEST AND WORST OF TV SHOWS

Rather than generate two other versions of Activity B.1   The Best Shows on TV, we will simply offer suggestions for doing so. The Application Activities that accompany this chapter ask the reader to act on these ideas.

Increase the Information Load

As formulated, groups of learners are assigned one of six sentences to complete in at least three ways. The easiest way to increase the information load is to increase the number of statements each group must work with from one to two or three. As seen in the higher-level activities for Activity A, having learners consider multiple perspectives increases the information load they handle. Activity B.1 focuses only on the best shows; this perspective could be augmented by a consideration of not only the best but also the worst shows. Activity B.1 allows for shows to be named from either the past or present. Another way, then, to increase the information load is to require that shows be named from the past as well as from the present. Other possibilities for increasing the information load of Activity B.1 include discussing animated versus nonanimated shows; exploring differences between major network and cable programs; examining adult versus family-oriented programming; or examining daytime versus evening programming.

Explore More Subtopics or More Complex Subtopics

Evolving Activity B.1 toward higher levels of instruction could also involve exploring more subtopics as well as more complex subtopics. A more complex subtopic will require the learners to examine TV shows using the framework of popularity. For example, they could address the question, What are the best and worst of the most popular shows on TV? The learners might also explore generational differences. They could respond for themselves and their age group, then respond for their parents. Following are some of the possibilities for exploring more complex subtopics in higher-level versions of Activity B.1.

- Police dramas
- Situation comedies
- Soap operas
- Shows that focus on families and family relationships

- Shows that focus on the workplace and work relationships
- Shows whose lead character is a married female
- Shows whose lead character is a single/divorced female
- Shows whose lead character is a married male
- Shows whose lead character is a single/divorced male

The final step of Activity B.1 is to provide examples of shows that fit the characteristics presented. The cognitive demands of the activity will increase if the class first names its favorite shows and then analyzes them for their treatment of different groups. The learners are, in essence, placed in the position of defending their viewing habits rather than speaking in general, idealized terms about shows they may or may not watch. Following are some of the possibilities for making the tasks more cognitively demanding in higher-level versions of Activity B.1.

- Analyze specific shows rather than merely name shows as examples.
- Consider the positive and negative aspects of specific shows.
- Contrast shows about working-class people with shows about the rich.

Alter the Way Linguistic Support Is Provided

In Activity A.3, learners were provided sentence-level grammatical support for exploring a more complex subtopic. Instructors should never hesitate to offer linguistic support to language learners of all levels—beginning, intermediate, or advanced. As was so clear in the Poor Claudia exchange Leeman Guthrie analyzed (Excerpt 6 in Chapter 2), the instructor responded inappropriately by chastising Claudia for forgetting the two ways she had already studied to express "pride." Increasing the information and cognitive loads in activities for more advanced learners may necessitate providing them linguistic support for sentence-level production. Exactly what types of linguistic support would be needed or appropriate for an activity can only be generated as the activity is written. (The Application Activities for this chapter include an activity that asks you to develop these activities.) There is, therefore, no list of ideas that can be generated at this time.

IMPLEMENTING INTERACTION AT HIGHER LEVELS OF INSTRUCTION

To demonstrate how the instructor's role evolves at higher levels of instruction, we offer suggestions for orchestrating the instructional events that make up Activities A.2 and A.3. The four components of orchestrating an instructional event presented in Chapter 5 will be used here: framing, executing, timing, and concluding. When orchestrating instructional events at the second- and third-year levels, instructors should be keenly conscious of and constantly working toward speaking as little as possible. As learners' language abilities increase, so should their opportunities for using the language. Importantly, as the instructional level increases, so should the learners' responsibility for executing the instructional event. The decisions an instructor makes for higher levels of instruction must account for these two factors.

Activity A.2   More Physically or More Mentally Active?

Framing

The instructor can write the phrase "last week" on the board and then include the phrases, "mental activity" and "physical activity."

LAST WEEK

mental activity   physical activity

A conscious decision was made in this book to narrate ways to implement the activities, as if an instructor were speaking to a class. The alternative was to describe in paragraphs these various suggestions. The narratives give more life to the activities than descriptions allow. They might also help instructors learn to project themselves into the classroom while they select and sequence materials. A technique that some instructors use in planning is to visualize themselves implementing an activity. Some instructors go as far as this book does and script a narrative they might follow in the classroom.

He or she can introduce the purpose of the activity by highlighting the outcome of the activity.

I: In this activity you will have to interview a partner about what he or she did last week. Then we will determine if last week was more mentally active [*underlines "mental activity" on the board*] or more physically active [*underlines "physical activity" on the board*] for the class as a whole.

Executing and Timing

Step 1 involves announcing that the interactional pattern is to work individually and that the time limit for completing the step is 1 minute.

I: I want you to do Step 1. You will not need any more than a minute. Begin.

Step 2 is similar in that the instructor need do no more than direct the learners to work in groups and to do the step in 5 minutes.

I: Time is up. Now get in groups of two or three. Check your answers on Step 1 and then do Step 2. It will take at most five minutes. Go ahead and get in groups now. [*Monitors groups to ensure that their lists of activities include half that are more mental than physical.*]

Since Step 3 requires exchanging information at the whole-class level, the instructor needs to establish a mechanism for doing so. The purpose of Step 3 is to build an information base for the interview in Step 4. The products of group interaction are incorporated into the activity; the group work is, therefore, not gratuitous. Every group in the class can be asked to read its list, thereby assuring that everyone participates. Having every single group report is not, however, a very efficient way to manage time. The instructor can instead ask for three groups to volunteer to present their lists of activities. As each subsequent group presents, it is asked to name only activities that are novel, that have not yet been named. After the three groups present, the instructor can ask anyone in the class for activities that have not yet been named. The technique of asking for novel information encourages the class to listen to each other. They will have to listen in order not to repeat what has already been presented.

I: Time is up. Let's see what you came up with. I need three groups to volunteer. [*Selects from among raised hands.*] OK. As each group tells us what they have on their lists, the rest of you should be adding to your lists. Take notes. OK? Group 1. What do you have on your list? Also tell us if the activity is mentally or physically active. [*Group 1 reports.*] Group 2. Tell us what you have that is different. Don't repeat any activities we have already heard. [*Group 2 reports.*] Now Group 3. What do you have that we have not yet heard? [*Group 3 reports.*] Now, does anyone in the class have an activity that has not yet been mentioned? [*Individuals offer activities.*]

The information exchange required in Step 4 is pivotal to the structure of the activity. Steps 1 through 3 have led to this interview and Step 5 asks learners to reach a conclusion based on the information exchanged. The learners are moving from group work to pair work, so the instructor must establish how the pairing should take place. To maximize the amount of information each person in the pairing has had access to, the pair can consist of learners who did not work together in groups. After the instructor announces the mechanism for pairing and the time limit, he or she can step back and prepare for Step 5.

I: Now that you have these different activities to draw on, you need to interview someone about what he or she did last week. You need to work in pairs. You have to work with someone from a different group. From a different group from the one you worked in on Step 2. I will give you at most 10 minutes to pair off and do the interview. Begin.

While the learners interview each other, the instructor can return to the visual used to frame the activity and write the scale underneath each of the activity categories.

LAST WEEK

	Mental Activity				Physical Activity		
Very	Somewhat		Not at all	Very		Somewhat	Not at all
1	2	3	4	5	1	2	3	4	5

When the interviewing is complete, the instructor should announce that each person should evaluate his or her partner's activities. Then the instructor can collect the results of the interviews by tallying responses. This technique was suggested for executing the final step of Activity A.1. The tallying can proceed by first asking the learners to answer for their partner and then moving from number to number on each scale, asking for a show of hands.

I: Time! Look at the scales in Step 5. Take what you learned about your partner and make two assessments, one for mental activity and one for physical activity. I'll give you a minute to do it. [*One minute elapses.*] Let's tally these and find out what kind of week we had last week. Let's do mentally active first. How many rated their partner with a 1? [*Writes tally on the board.*] How many rated their partner with a 2? [*Writes tally on the board.*] With a 3? [*Writes tally on the board.*] 4? [*Writes tally on the board.*] 5? [*Writes tally on the board.*] Now let's do physically active. How many rated their partner with a 1? [*Writes tally on the board.*] How many rated their partner with a 2? [*Writes tally on the board.*] With a 3? [*Writes tally on the board.*] 4? [*Writes tally on the board.*] 5? [*Writes tally on the board.*]

Concluding

The suggestions offered for concluding Activity A.1 at the first-year level required the instructor to engage in a good deal of speaking because the instructor drew the activity to its conclusion. At higher levels of instruction, the learners can be made more responsible for concluding activities: The instructor can physically step away from the board and move into the area where the learners are seated. From that vantage point, the instructor can direct the learners to look at the numbers and declare whether the class as a whole was more mentally or more physically active last week.

I: [*Sits down in the back of the classroom among the students.*] Well, what do you think? Was last week more mentally active or more physically active? What conclusion can we come to about ourselves? I want each of you to examine the numbers on the board. Then, each of you should take 2 minutes to write a sentence that starts "In conclusion." Begin. [*Two minutes elapse.*] Let's have a volunteer read their sentence. Paul. [*Learner reads sentence.*] How many of you agree with Paul? Raise your hands. Most of you. Jenny, you didn't raise your hand. Would you read your sentence?

SUMMARY

Previous work has approached the question of curricular sequencing in a variety of ways. In this chapter we have taken a cognitive approach to developing activities for non-beginning levels of language instruction as opposed to a purely linguistic one. Using the activities presented in Chapter 3 as a springboard, two higher-level activities were developed around the three criteria of increasing the information load, exploring more subtopics and more complex subtopics, and altering the way linguistic support is provided as the means by which to make the tasks more cognitively demanding. Ideas were given for developing higher-level activities based on Activity B.1. Finally, suggestions were given for orchestrating the interaction for Activities A.2 and A.3.

GAINING GREATER PERSPECTIVE

1. *Curricular Sequencing.* There are many approaches to curricular sequencing. VanPatten (1987) presents a curricular sequence from a second language acquisition perspective. In particular, he traces the roles of input and output across beginning, intermediate, and advanced levels of language learners. Omaggio Hadley (1986, 1993) uses the ACTFL Proficiency Guidelines to frame her discussion of language instruction. Nunan's (1991, pp. 113–115) graded activity specifications for beginning, pre-intermediate, and intermediate learners parallel the Guidelines in their structure. Omaggio Hadley and Brown and Palmer (1988) offer concrete classroom activities that exemplify different levels. The latter classify the activities they present in Chapter 6 as first day of class, first week, first term, and higher terms; this classification is more experientially based rather than driven by the application of a set of principles. All the same, it does illustrate an approach to curricular sequencing.

2. *Issues.* Candlin (1987) offers a long list of considerations in an article that is mostly "issue raising," as he terms it. A few of the issues he raises overlap with those presented in this chapter, and so, many of the considerations important to Candlin will provide greater perspective on the issues surrounding curricular sequencing and developing tasks appropriate for higher levels of language learners.

APPLICATION ACTIVITIES

1. Write a script demonstrating how you would orchestrate the interaction for Activity A.3   Mentally and Physically Active. Be sure to include all elements important to this discussion: framing, executing, timing, concluding, and evolving the instructor's role.

2. Develop two activities for higher levels of instruction based on Activity B.1   The Best Shows on TV. Various ideas are presented in the chapter that can guide your thinking, but you should feel free to propose something not suggested in the chapter.

3. Write a script demonstrating how you would orchestrate the interaction that could be engendered by the new activities you developed for Activity B.1. Be sure to include all elements important to this discussion: framing, executing, timing, concluding, and evolving the instructor's role.

4. Develop alternate versions for higher levels of Activity Bilingual and Bicultural presented in Chapter 4. Then write a script that demonstrates how you would orchestrate the interaction for each activity.

CHAPTER 7

Building Language Competence Through Task-Based Activities

CHAPTER OVERVIEW

Although the focus of this book is on exploring the relationship between tasks and communication, tasks also offer a framework for developing language competence in learners. It is important to note that language competence is not simply grammatical competence. It is a broader construct that includes not only grammatical competence but also illocutionary competence and textual competence. In this chapter we explore how task-based activities can be used to develop language competence. The two activities presented in Chapter 3 will be analyzed to see how they promote the development of illocutionary competence and textual competence. Suggestions are offered for enhancing how task-based activities can develop grammatical competence.

COMMUNICATIVE LANGUAGE ABILITY

Canale and Swain (1980) proposed a widely accepted and heavily cited model of communicative competence that, as Brown indicates, is "now the reference point for virtually all discussions of communicative competence vis-à-vis second language teaching" (Brown 1987, p. 199). Notable work with the model followed (Canale 1980; Savignon 1983, 1997). The model comprises the following subcomponent competences: strategic competence, discourse competence, sociolinguistic competence, and grammatical competence. Many scholars and researchers have examined these competencies in more detail: strategic competence (Tarone 1984; Swaffar et al. 1992); discourse competence (Kramsch 1993); sociolinguistic competence (Byrnes 1991; Kramsch 1991); and grammatical competence (Omaggio 1986; Omaggio Hadley 1994). Bachman's (1990) theoretical framework for communicative language ability is perhaps one of the most comprehensive syntheses of work done under the rubric of communicative competence. Bachman builds on Canale and Swain's model as well as those of others, refining descriptions, categories, mechanisms, and the interrelation-

TABLE 7.1. Components of Language Competence

Organizational Competence	Grammatical	vocabulary, morphology, syntax, phonology, graphemics
	Textual	cohesion, rhetorical organization
Pragmatic Competence	Illocutionary	functions: ideational, manipulative, heuristic, imaginative
	Sociolinguistic	sensitivities to: dialect, variety, register, naturalness, cultural references, figures of speech

Source: Adapted from Bachman 1990, p. 87.

ships among them. Adopting the term "communicative language ability" over "communicative competence," he describes communicative language ability

> "as both knowledge of language and the capacity for implementing that knowledge in communicative language use. . . . Communicative language ability consists of language competence, strategic competence, and psychophysiological mechanisms. Language competence includes organizational competence, which consists of grammatical and textual competence, and pragmatic competence, which consists of illocutionary and sociolinguistic competence. Strategic competence is seen as the capacity that relates language competence, or knowledge of language, to the language user's knowledge structures and the features of the context in which communication takes place" (1990, p. 107).

Important in the definition Bachman provides is that communicative language ability is both the knowledge learners have of the language and the capacity for acting on that knowledge. Table 7.1 displays the components of language competence as Bachman has formulated them.

The purpose of this chapter is to make explicit connections between task-based language learning activities and building language competence through task-based interaction. The pedagogy thus far described in this book has focused on instructor-learner and learner-learner interactions but has not united that pedagogy with a more global or complete pedagogy of language instruction. The questions remain as yet unanswered, How can language competence be taught as part of a pedagogy that has moved learner-to-learner interaction into center stage? Where and how does instruction oriented toward language competence fit into the instructional events described in previous chapters?

It is important to keep in mind that the communicative language ability we want to develop in second language learners is the communicative language ability native speakers of the "second language" have. That is, communicative language ability in Japanese is different from

A rather simple association many instructors make is to equate the terms *language* and *grammar*. Although we refer to ourselves as language teachers, many restrict themselves to being grammar teachers. Language is presented and explored in this chapter along many dimensions, of which grammar is only one.

communicative language ability in Arabic. Although discourse competence, for example, is a universal aspect of communicative language ability, a native speaker of Japanese does not construct discourse in the same way as does a native speaker of Arabic. A native English-speaker learning Japanese or Arabic must learn to construct discourse in a Japanese- or Arabic-appropriate way.

A COMPUTING, ON-LINE PERSPECTIVE

To use an example familiar to many, picture what happens when you create a new document on a Macintosh computer using Microsoft Word. All the while, you are viewing a toolbar of twenty-six icons, a ribbon of thirty-four icons, and a ruler across the top of the computer screen. Whenever you click on an icon, something happens. For example, the icon that contains the letters A, B, and C, and a checkmark offers a dictionary against which to check word spellings. You can check individual words, sentences, paragraphs, or the entire document. The icon that contains an upside-down question mark and an accented a (á) offers a menu of symbols and letters containing diacritics. The desired one is selected, and it is inserted in the text at the spot where the cursor is blinking. At the same time, files containing other documents can be open in the window. When you need to check a reference, presence or absence of a concept, or the phrasing of a particular point, you can access the other documents in the window. All the operations and information these icons represent are *support mechanisms.* They *support* the principal task at hand, which is to write the new document. When we *want* or *need* the support the computer offers, we *access* it.

Let's consider a computer program designed for second language reading rather than word processing. The principal activity the learners carry out is that of comprehending written text. To do so, they may require support. Many computer programs offer an online dictionary of some sort. If learners/readers do not know a word in the text, they can highlight or click on it and call up the dictionary. Some programs have options built into this request for help with meaning. Learners might first be offered a definition of the word in the target language. If they cannot construct meaning from the target language definition, they might then be offered target language synonyms and antonyms for the selected word. If they still cannot construct meaning from these, they might finally be offered the equivalent term in their native language. If the learners need or want help with word meaning, they can access it as well as accessing different types of help.

The two examples, word processing and second language reading, underscore the point that there is a principal event taking place for which various types and kinds of support are offered when needed or wanted. We can extrapolate from these examples to classroom language instruction. The principal event taking place in the classroom is the expression, interpretation, and negotiation of meaning, also known as *communication.* There are various types and kinds of support we can offer language learners when needed or wanted, and the support falls under the rubric of building language competence. How can the subcomponent competences of language competence be built in such a way as to support communication, the principal event in the classroom? This question guides the presentation of ideas in the remainder of this chapter. As you read subsequent sections, consider the pedagogy of language competence as you would help-boxes in a computer program: important and useful but not central.

ILLOCUTIONARY COMPETENCE

The *illocutionary force of communication* refers to the function, purpose, and intent with which we use language. We use language to bring about some effect. Brown provides four excellent examples.

> " 'I can't find my umbrella,' uttered by a frustrated adult who is late for work on a rainy day, may be a frantic request for all in the household to join in a search. The child who says 'I want some ice cream' is rarely stating a simple fact or observation but requesting ice cream in her own intimate register. A sign on the street that says 'one way' functions to guide traffic in only one direction. A sign in a church parking lot in a busy downtown area was subtle in form but direct in function: 'We forgive those who trespass against us, but we also tow them'; that sign functioned effectively to prevent unauthorized cars from parking in the lot" (Brown 1987, p. 202).

Bachman (1990, p. 92) incorporates four illocutionary functions of language into his model. First is *ideational*, which refers to expressing meaning in terms of our experience in the real world. For example, an adult who has tried a new flavor of ice cream relates to another, "Rocky Mocha Banana ice cream is delicious. After I tried it, I bought a half gallon." Second is *manipulative*, which refers to expressing meaning in order to affect the world around us, to get things done, or to control the behavior of others. For example, the person who received the information about Rocky Mocha Banana ice cream might respond, "I think I would like that flavor. Is that half gallon in the freezer?" as a means of eliciting an offer of some ice cream from the first speaker. Then there is the *heuristic* function, through which we extend our knowledge of the world around us. It is language used to acquire knowledge. Questions can function heuristically: Asking "Where can you buy Rocky Mocha Banana ice cream?" is an example of the heuristic function of language. Finally, there is the *imaginative* function of language, through which we create or extend our world for humorous (joking) or aesthetic (poetry) purposes. Although we can identify separate illocutionary functions and analyze speech accordingly, we must be aware that most language, especially language in discourse, often performs several functions *simultaneously*. The question "Is it in the freezer?" may be both manipulative and heuristic. It is heuristic because the answer gives information to the speaker, but manipulative when the intent is to elicit an offer of a serving of ice cream.

Language Use/Functions Required by Different Tasks

It should go without saying that language learners should be provided opportunities to use language to function in all four ways. To develop illocutionary

TABLE 7.2. Task Demands and Illocutionary Functions of the Steps in Activity A.1. What Did You Do Last Week?

Task Demands	Primary Illocutionary Functions
Step 1: Categorize activities; verify categorization with class	ideational; manipulative
Step 2: List and categorize activities; verify categorization with class	ideational; manipulative
Step 3: Interview partner	ideational; manipulative; heuristic
Step 4: Categorize set of activities; rate the week of activities	ideational
Step 5: Profile the class as a whole	ideational; heuristic

TABLE 7.3. Task Demands and Illocutionary Functions of the Steps in Activity B.1. The Best Shows on TV

Task Demand	Illocutionary Functions
Step 1: Groups complete sentences	ideational; manipulative
Step 2: Present sentence completions; note others' completions; agree or disagree with those completions	ideational; manipulative; heuristic
Step 3: Give examples of programs	ideational

competence, language learners need to be provided a variety of contexts in which to use language. Tables 7.2 and 7.3 present the multiple illocutionary functions found in the activities presented in Chapter 3.

Specifying Communication Goals

In some approaches to communicative language teaching, learners may not be aware of what they are learning or how they are learning it (Lee 1989). It becomes necessary, then, to be explicit. In Chapters 5 and 6 we provided suggestions for implementing interaction in communicative classrooms. One suggestion offered was to frame each activity with a statement that illuminates the outcome of the activity, the outcome being the communicative goal of the activity. The suggestion was to announce the goal to the learners as a way to introduce the activity—to be explicit from the outset about where the activity will end so that learners will be aware of what they are learning. The illocutionary or communication goals of the activities developed in this book are given in Table 7.4. Instructors can use these goal statements to introduce the activities and help learners be aware of the different ways in which they will be using language in the classroom.

Activity	Illocutionary or Communication Goals
A.1 What Did You Do Last Week?	To profile the type of week the class as a whole had last week
A.2 More Physically or More Mentally Active?	To profile whether the class as a whole was more physically or more mentally active last week
A.3 Mentally and Physically Active	To propose both mental and physical dimensions of activities
B.1 The Best Shows on TV	To characterize the treatment of various peoples and groups on the best shows on TV and to provide examples of such shows

Follow-Up Discussion Questions

The approach to task-based activities presented in this book organizes the activity into a series of discrete steps. Within each step, learners carry out at least one task, sometimes more. The tasks engage learners in purposeful language use. Completing a series of tasks allows learners to achieve a communication goal. Additionally, the task-based activity can act as a common information base from which the learners can draw in order to discuss relevant topics, issues, and ideas. The ideas presented in Table 7.5 are suggestions for following up Activities A.1 and B.1 with discussion questions. Moreover, the questions are grouped by illocutionary function so as to underscore how these questions contribute to developing the learners' language competence.

TEXTUAL COMPETENCE

As Bachman points out (1990, p. 89), conversational language use gives rise to the necessity of organizing discourse. When speakers organize their discourse, they do so in ways that are appropriate to the language use context and in ways that efficiently achieve their communicative goals. Textual competence concerns both these means by which speakers organize their discourse. We will concern ourselves in this section with two aspects of textual competence, *cohesion* and *rhetorical organization*. *Cohesion* involves the conventions for stringing utterances together to form a single text or message. Explicitly marking semantic

Even in our native languages, we are not all equally adept at communicating our ideas, participating in conversations, or getting others to participate in conversations. Instructors cannot simply assume that learners will transfer what they know about communicating in their first language to a second language context. Considerations of culturally appropriate patterns of communication aside, learners need to be given the tools to help them communicate. Just as the approach to task-based instruction in this book advocates providing linguistic support, it also advocates providing communicative support.

TABLE 7.5. Follow-Up Discussion Questions Grouped by Illocutionary Function

Activity	Function	Discussion Questions
A.1 What Did You Do Last Week?	ideational	Do you agree with your partner's assessment of your week? Does the class profile match yours?
	manipulative	What recommendations can you make to very active or very sedentary people so that they bring some balance into their lives? What are the advantages and disadvantages of an active lifestyle? of a sedentary one?
	heuristic	Did you already know what kind of week your partner might have had? Was the class profile a surprise or was it predictable based on what you already know about these people?
	imaginative	Can you create a set of activities for an imaginary person whose week would be classified as either very sedentary or very active? The profile should be so exaggerated as to entertain your classmates.
B.1 The Best Shows on TV	ideational	How many of the shows that the class came up with have you watched? Are some better than others? Are any of them personal favorites?
	manipulative	What arguments can you come up with to convince people that they should watch these shows? How would you convince someone to stop watching a show that presented negative images of any of the groups of people mentioned in Step 1?
	heuristic	Will you watch some of the shows you have not seen before? Which ones?
	imaginative	Could you create a new show by combining two or three of the shows mentioned? Would this be a comical program, dramatic, or educational?

relationships and ordering old and new information in discourse are two examples of cohesion. The aspect of textual competence termed *rhetorical organization* refers to the overall conceptual structure of a message. It includes how we develop narratives, descriptions, comparisons, classifications, and so on. Additionally, rhetorical organization includes such conversational conventions as topic nomination and development, topic shifts, and conversation maintenance. In the remainder of this section, we offer examples of discourse conventions and devices that can be offered to language learners to help them achieve their communicative goals in ways appropriate to the language use context.

TABLE 7.6. The Discourse Subsumed in the Activities

A.1	to present
	to agree/disagree
	to interview
	to profile
A.2	to present
	to interview
	to profile
A.3	to present
	to propose
	to conclude
B.1	to present
	to agree/disagree
	to characterize
	to provide examples

Cohesion and Coherence

Table 7.4 provided statements that overtly identified the communication goals of several of the activities included in this book. In order to help language learners meet these communicative goals, we can suggest ways in which they might explicitly mark semantic relationships as well as order old and new information, thereby adding cohesion and coherence to their spoken language. In Table 7.6 you will find the discourse subsumed by the various steps of the activities. What conventions of language use explicitly mark information as an example? What language overtly marks that a contrast is being made or that differences between entities are being expressed? How do speakers indicate that they are stating the characteristics of an entity? How can speakers signal that they are making a conclusion?

Providing Examples

The communication goal for Activity B.1 is to provide examples of programs from the past and present that fit the criteria established in the first steps of the activity. The conventions in Figure 7.1 explicitly mark the information that follows them as examples. Utilizing either of these conventions will result in cohesive and coherent discourse because the speaker will identify for the listener how the information is to be understood.

Stating Characteristics

To meet the communication goal of Activity B.1, the speaker must be able to characterize the treatment of various groups of people. The conventions presented in Figure 7.2 explicitly mark the information in the utterance as a characteristic. Listeners will be able to take in the information much more efficiently and effectively if the speaker uses such conventions to mark the information.

Arriving at a Conclusion

Activity A.3 requires learners to evaluate the tenor and direction of their discussion in order to come to a conclusion. The conventions in Figure 7.3 explicitly mark the information in the utterance as a conclusion.

In this activity you will provide examples to illustrate your criteria. You can use the following words and phrases to help your listeners understand better the points you want to make.

For example, . . . Another example . . . . Finally, . . .

I can give three examples. First, . . . Second, . . . Third, . . .

MODEL: *I can give* three examples of women on TV. *First,* Murphy Brown. *Second,* Ellen. *Third,* Mary Tyler Moore. All of these women are professionals.

FIGURE 7.1 Discourse Markers for Providing Examples

In this activity you will talk about the characteristics of television shows, in particular, their treatment of various groups of people. The following words and phrases will help you do that and make your message more easily understood by others.

is/are characterized by

consists of

The characteristics of . . . are . . .

MODEL: The best shows on TV do not present women as victims. These shows *are characterized by* professional women. They *consist of* characters who have good relationships, good friends, and good futures.

FIGURE 7.2 Discourse Markers for Stating Characteristics

In this activity you will evaluate the things said in order for each an appropriate conclusion. To help your listeners know that your statement is a conclusion, you can use the following words and phrases.

In conclusion,

Given everything said,

After all is said and done,

So, in the end,

Based on our discussion,

MODEL: *Given everything said,* it seems easier to add physical activity to mental ones.

FIGURE 7.3 Discourse Markers for Concluding

In this activity you interview a classmate. If you don't understand what is said, try to let your partner know just what you missed. For example, try repeating back to your partner what you have understood or what you think you have understood.

—I played tennis XXXX times last week.
—I'm sorry. You played tennis two times last week?

—I played XXXX three times last week.
—You played what three times last week?

FIGURE 7.4 Signaling Misunderstanding

Rhetorical Organization

The aspect of textual competence called *rhetorical organization* concerns such features of discourse as topic nomination, topic development, and conversation maintenance. In this section, we focus on conversation maintenance because, on the one hand, this feature of discourse is more commonly taught, and on the other, the step-by-step structure of the activities function to nominate and develop topics.

Signaling Misunderstanding

Misunderstandings arise for any number of reasons, only one of which is the limited language ability that characterizes language learners. Sometimes we just do not hear what the other person has said. Other times, our attention lapses and we find that we have tuned out the other person. Many instructors and materials developers suggest to learners that they can ask for repetition and provide them the words and phrases to do so. Asking for repetition of an entire idea is a way of not accepting responsibility for one's own comprehension. It is rare that a learner has not understood an entire message but might have understood some of the words used in the message. To accept responsibility for one's misunderstanding involves signaling to the speaker what specific part of the message was misunderstood. To that end, learners can be provided strategies for managing their interactions with others. For all three versions of Activity A What Did You Do Last Week?, learners must interview each other. How can they signal to the person they are interviewing that they have not completely understood something? Suggestions are given in Figure 7.4.

Involving Others in the Discussion

All the task-based activities presented in this book require language learners to interact with each other in paired, group, or whole-class interactional patterns. Importantly, the products of this paired and grouped interaction *are* utilized in subsequent steps of the activity. In other words, the learners do not engage in gratuitous group work. An underlying assumption that should now be made explicit is that, within the group, no one learner should dominate. No one learner should take on the sole responsibility for creating the information. Rather, each participant must be given equal footing in the interaction. In most classes, the stronger students take the lead and the success of an activity may rest on the fact that there are such leaders. To prevent some learners from

> It is important for everyone in a group to participate. Everyone should be given the opportunity to use the second language to communicate. Sometimes people's participation needs to be encouraged. Here are some ways to encourage others' involvement in the discussion.
>
> What do you think?
>
> Do you agree with me/us?
>
> Do you want to add something?
>
> Can you think of another example?
>
> Are you satisfied with the list?
>
> Will you report this to the class?
>
> Will you take notes for the group?

FIGURE 7.5 Involving Others in the Discussion

dominating their classmates, these leaders must be provided some strategies and techniques for turning the discourse over to others. The most appreciated and esteemed quality of their leadership should be their ability to involve, not shut out, others in a discussion. Figure 7.5 presents a means for accomplishing that goal.

GRAMMATICAL COMPETENCE

In a series of writings (1988, 1991, 1993, 1996), VanPatten explains that the question surrounding grammar instruction has been unfortunately framed as whether to teach grammar. He advocates instead that the question should be, How do we teach grammar so as to maximize the benefits of instruction? And so, the question that frames the present discussion of grammatical competence is, How can grammar instruction support the expression, interpretation, and negotiation of meaning? In other words, Can grammar instruction be consistent with a focus on interaction?

Adopting the perspective that grammar should support communication leads to questioning what grammar the learners need to complete an activity. Let's take Activity A.1 as an example. The learners need to express events that took place in the past. Each learner needs to express what he or she did as well as question what a classmate did. The learners need, therefore, only two forms of the verb, first- and second-person singular. Moreover, each learner needs to ask a classmate what he or she did last week. The learners will benefit from being given the appropriate syntactic and morphological configurations for questions about the past. The following two grammar notes (Figures 7.6 and 7.7) serve the purpose of providing language learners the linguistic support they need in order to carry out Activity A.1.

Activity B.1 would also be made more effective by providing linguistic support to the learners via a grammar note. In Step 1, the learners must complete sentences that utilize the following basic structure.

Forms
The simple past tense is formed by adding *-ed* to the end of the present tense form of the verb.

I walked	we walked	I played	we played
you walked	you walked	you played	you played
he/she, it walked	they walked	he/she, it played	they played

Function
To indicate that an event took place in the past

FIGURE 7.6 **Grammar Note** The Past Tense, Regular Verbs

Forms
In questions, the past tense is formed using *did*, the past tense of the verb *do*, plus the present tense form of the verb.

did walk   did play
did talk   did wash

Syntax
The following pattern characterizes the syntax of past tense questions.

    did + *subject* + *verb* + *other sentence elements*

Did you play tennis last week?

Did you wash clothes last week?

Did you talk to the instructor last week?

Did you walk five miles last week?

Function
To question what took place in the past

FIGURE 7.7 **Grammar Note** The Past Tense, Question Formation

   noun + *aux.* + **not** + *verb* + *noun* + **as** + _____

   The best shows on TV do not present women as _____ .

Even though the beginning part of the sentence serves as linguistic support, instructors can also offer learners other grammatically relevant information. For example, the part of speech required by this sentence structure is a noun, not an adjective. Also, instructors might offer information on negation, since negating the sentence

   The best shows on TV present women as _____ .

requires the auxiliary *do* to precede the negator, which must precede the main verb.

LIMITS OF CLASSROOM DISCOURSE: SOCIOLINGUISTIC COMPETENCE

Under the rubric of sociocultural competence, instructors have labored to teach learners politeness formulae and conversational management. As Kramsch (1991) points out, that is a reductionist approach to what discourse is. She underscores that the concept of "language use in social contexts" has misled teachers into separating language from the conceptual schemata that language creates, the conceptual terrain in which knowledge is formed and produced through language" (p. 192). Referring to ordinary foreign language classrooms as sociolinguistically impoverished, Valdman (1992) asserts that "even with the most ingenious *simulated* natural use of language it is impossible to create suitable conditions for the contextualized use of language among nonnative speakers in a classroom environment" (p. 80; emphasis added).

The sensitivities Bachman includes in sociolinguistic competence are sensitivities to dialect, variety, register, and naturalness. Developing these sensitivities requires language learners to have contact with native speakers of varying ages, professions or occupations, ethnicities, and national origins. It also requires language learners to have this type of contact in a variety of settings, such as a group of friends at a café, a formal family meal, a study group of fellow students, a dialogue with a professor, a store clerk, or a travel agent. Although not always practical, such native speakers can be asked to participate in certain classes and carry out task-based activities as one of the group members. The presence of these native speakers will certainly have a great impact on the interaction; whether it is feasible to bring them into the classroom is another issue. But more important, any interaction that takes place in the classroom among these participants will only *simulate* a possible nonclassroom interaction.

SUMMARY

In this chapter we examined language competence as one aspect of developing communicative language ability, focusing on the subcomponent processes to organizational and pragmatic competences. We used the idea of on-line help boxes for providing learners information they might need to express, interpret, and negotiate meaning. The model activities used in previous chapters of this book were analyzed repeatedly throughout this chapter. Under the heading of illocutionary competence, we first presented the illocutionary functions of the language elicited in each step of Activities A.1, A.2, A.3, and B.1. Second, we provided statements of the communication goals of each activity. Finally, we proposed follow-up discussion questions organized around each of the four illocutionary functions. Under the heading of textual competence, we first presented suggestions for providing phrases and words that will help speakers create cohesive and coherent discourse. Second, we suggested ways for learners to maintain their conversations. Under the heading of grammatical competence, we proposed the grammar note as a way of expanding on how to provide linguistic support in an activity. The chapter ended with a brief statement concerning the difficulty of developing sociolinguistic competence in classrooms.

GAINING GREATER PERSPECTIVE

1. *Communicative Competence.* Two very readable works that apply communicative competence to language teaching are Canale and Swain (1980) and Savignon (1997).
2. *Grammar.* How best to develop the grammatical competence of language learners? Many have addressed this question in one form or another. Some interesting works on this topic include VanPatten (1991)—in particular, the section titled "How Grammar Fits into a Communication-Based Curriculum." Fotos and Ellis (1991) offer a task-based approach related to grammar instruction.
3. *Communication Strategies.* Many textbooks have incorporated communication strategies into the pedagogy, sometimes as a part of the fabric of instruction, sometimes as an addendum. Several models exist that would be worth investigating further: Chastain and Guntermann (1987), Galloway and LaBarca (1993), VanPatten et al. (1996), and Lee et al. (1996).
4. *Cross-Cultural Communicative Competence.* A work that examines the potential of task-based approaches to instruction in order to develop cross-cultural communicative competence has yet to be written. Many educators have begun to frame the issues that will have to be taken into account. Kramsch (1993) presents a cogent argument regarding culture and context in language teaching. Others who have made strides in this area include Byrnes (1991) and Swaffar (1992). Omaggio Hadley (1993) includes a chapter on teaching for cultural understanding, the bibliography for which (pp. 407–411) offers many titles to explore further.

APPLICATION ACTIVITIES

1. How do learners use language? Identify the illocutionary functions of the various steps that comprise the following.
   a. Activity Bilingualism and Biculturalism (Chapter 4)
   b. The higher-level versions of Activity B.1 (if you developed them as part of the Application Activities in Chapter 6)
2. What is the illocutionary or communication goal of each activity? Look at the final steps of each of the following activities and write out the communication goals.
   a. Activity Bilingualism and Biculturalism (Chapter 4)
   b. The higher-level versions of Activity B.1 (if you developed them as part of the Application Activities in Chapter 6)
3. Develop follow-up discussion questions for the following activities. Try to pose questions for each of the four illocutionary functions presented in this chapter.
   a. Activities A.2 and A.3 (Chapter 6)

   b. Activity Bilingualism and Biculturalism (Chapter 4)

   c. The higher-level versions of Activity B.1 (if you developed them as part of the Application Activities in Chapter 6)

4. If you teach a language other than English, develop the grammatical support needed for Activities A.1 and B.1. Follow the model of the grammar notes presented in this chapter.

5. Step 4 of Activity A.3 (Chapter 6) offers learners morphosyntactic linguistic support. Develop the necessary grammatical support (grammar note) for the if/then statements. If the language you teach requires a different morphosyntactic structure, develop the grammatical support necessary for that language.

6. Develop grammatical support for the following.

   a. Activity Bilingualism and Biculturalism (Chapter 4)

   b. The higher-level versions of Activity B.1 (if you developed them as part of the Application Activities in Chapter 6)

CHAPTER 8

Task-Based Classroom Testing

CHAPTER OVERVIEW

We should not attempt to discuss testing without first having established the parameters and principles that guide what and how we teach. The previous chapters have presented communicative language teaching via a task-based approach to structuring interaction. That presentation must necessarily have preceded any formulation of communicative language testing. In this chapter, we make the critical link between instructional practices and test development by exploring how testing can support classroom practice and interacts with it, but not drive it. Once again we refer to the two activities presented in Chapter 3 to develop test sections from them. Two types of test sections are presented and discussed. First, we develop test sections that examine the specific content of the interactions that took place in class. Second, we develop test sections that parallel the mental process of in-class activities but do not test specific content. Issues surrounding this approach to testing are discussed.

POSITIVES AND NEGATIVES IN TEST DEVELOPMENT

Shohamy (1993) documents Israel as one case in which tests drove classroom practice. The state instituted national compulsory examinations, an act that, in and of itself, is neither good nor bad. The effect on teachers and publishers was immediate and, perhaps, a bit frenetic. Teachers began teaching toward the tests by developing materials that mirrored the formats found on the national examination. In other words, the tests did not open up their instructional practices, but limited and restricted them rather severely. The marketplace of commercially available materials almost overnight adopted the sales pitch that X, Y, and Z books, supplements, and other instructional materials prepared students for the national examinations. Shohamy's analysis of this case is not cynical, but rather even-handed. She does point to the benefits derived from imposing national examinations, such as an increase in the quality of instruction in certain sectors. Yet the title of her monograph, "The Power of Tests," clearly indicates both the up- and downsides of testing. Tests have the power to shape classroom practices, replace one practice with another, or, in the extreme, overturn a curriculum.

In actuality, the test itself has no power. Bachman (1990) points out that a test is a neutral instrument. A test is no more than a piece of paper with questions on it. The decisions people make based on test results, however, are not always neutral. A child who scores low on an IQ test in first grade may well be haunted by those results for many years to come as teachers, school administrators, and sometimes even parents use the score to make decisions about that child's schooling. Scores on college entrance examinations can have a profound impact on students' lives. People and institutions use those scores to make decisions that may either open up possibilities for the test-taker or limit them. Lee and VanPatten (1995) point out that, in the classroom context, some instructors may use test scores to decide whether the class has studied sufficiently or is keeping up with daily assignments. Some instructors use tests to confirm their feelings that a certain student is very dedicated or that another is disinterested and lazy. Are these appropriate decisions? Are these conclusions justified? Clearly, instructors must be careful to apply the power of tests to make appropriate decisions, to reach justifiable conclusions.

Instructors are not the only ones who are test-driven; learners are, too. Many undergraduates willingly reveal that their philosophy of class attendance centers around the tests; class attendance is particularly high the week a test is scheduled. If the material tested is "in the book," they view class attendance as something less than mandatory but more than optional. If they can gather the necessary information from the book, without the intervention of an instructor or instruction, they will. Most language instructors stress the importance of attendance and participation, but as abstract concepts—it's good for you, or you can't learn a language without practicing it—rather than as concrete constructs that directly affect learning. If a learner can score well on a language test without attending class, the learning behaviors are not enhancing language development (the assumption being that attending class is conducive to language development). The test is undermining the instructor's intent to promote learning behaviors that enhance language development.

Krashen and Terrell (1983) have long maintained that the best types of language tests encourage learners to engage in learning behaviors that enhance language development, not undermine it. By way of example, consider the essay versus multiple-choice test format. Learners do not engage in the same study behaviors for these two formats. Another example, more closely tied to language learning, should also demonstrate the point. Consider the following formats for testing vocabulary.

1. Give the English translation for each target language word.
2. For each of the following target language words, give a synonym and an antonym.
3. From among the four provided, select the target language word whose meaning does not fit with the meaning of the other three.

Giving the English translation of the target language word on the test leads learners to study each vocabulary word individually. They will be concerned only with the forms of the words, the native language form and its second language counterpart. The other two formats require learners to focus on the meanings of the vocabulary words and to relate the meanings of words to other vocabulary words. The learning behaviors associated with giving translations are completely inappropriate for these two formats.

Test formats can and do shape learning behaviors and they should, therefore, support in-class activity, not undermine it. We can use the power of tests to make learners responsible for what takes place in the classroom. An often repeated principle of testing is to test in ways consonant with what you teach and how you teach. Task-based instruction views language a bit differently. The definition of a task presented in Chapter 1 underscores the use of language as a means to an end: Tasks provide learners a purpose for using language. That purpose, as presented in the definition of communication, is to express, interpret, and negotiate meaning. Tests, then, should account for the purpose for which the learners used language in the classroom. Moreover, tests should also be communicative events: Learners should have opportunities to communicate via the testing formats. They should express, interpret, and negotiate meaning.

In the remainder of this chapter we will present a variety of test sections appropriate for use as classroom tests, derived from the task-based activities first presented in Chapter 3. Following are guidelines for developing these tests. Tests should:

- be neutral instruments
- be used by instructors to make appropriate decisions, since the power of a test rests on the instructor's decisions
- encourage appropriate learning behaviors, such as class participation
- make learners responsible for what happens in class
- incorporate formats that allow learners to express, interpret, and negotiate meaning

The remainder of the chapter is divided into three principal sections. In the first, we present formats that privilege the specific in-class interaction that results from carrying out specific task-based activities. Learners must have been present in class to carry out the test section. Subsequently, we discuss some issues surrounding this approach to testing and offer suggestions for addressing these issues. Since many would consider testing the content of in-class interactions a draconian measure, we subsequently present formats that privilege the mental processes underlying the classroom interaction. These formats reflect the type of thinking that takes place during the activity. By privileging the mental processes underlying the completion of an activity, an instructor makes a clear connection between classroom interaction and the test.

Even when instructors modify and develop their classroom practices, many fall back on familiar formats for testing language. Creativity with instructional materials does not always translate to creativity with testing materials. Although developing in-class activities for test sections may not seem very creative, it is an important first step in linking classroom and testing practices.

PRIVILEGING THE SPECIFIC CONTENT
OF IN-CLASS INTERACTION

On a scale of 1 to 5, with 1 being the least amount of learner responsibility and 5 being the greatest, test sections that privilege the specific content generated from in-class group interaction would receive a rating of 5. Responsibility rests with the learners, in that they are held accountable for their own participation in classroom activities. Success on the test can come only from attendance in class and active participation in activities. Test sections that privilege specific in-class interaction require that each learner have firsthand knowledge of the instructional event in order to complete the test section.

The rationale for linking test sections with specific in-class activities can be answered by addressing the question, How will learners prepare for tests that privilege the specific content of in-class interactions? To have anything to study outside class, learners must attend class and record the information generated in the various steps of the activities. The most appropriate out-of-class learning behavior will be to go over the results of the activities once again. This behavior is excellent from a language development point of view in that the learners are using the target language to learn the target language (which is the rationale for content language learning). Moreover, they are learning (practicing, reviewing) the vocabulary and grammar *in context* because they must be able to express, in their own words, what took place during the activity.

The following two test sections (1 A.1 and 2 B.1) have been derived from Activities A.1 and B.1. Both test sections utilize the same two-part structure. The first part of the test section requires the test-taker to recount the result of in-class group (small-group or whole-class) interaction. The second part calls for individual learners to comment on and evaluate the information recounted in the first part. Taken together, the two parts underscore both the learners' group membership and their individualities. In the first part of the test section, the learners recount information. In the second part, they provide a personal perspective on it.

Test Section 1 A.1   What Did You Do Last Week?   *Option 1*

Step 1. Compare/Contrast the rating you gave to your classmate's activities to the rating and profile we derived for the entire class. Be sure you give examples of his/her activities to support your answer.

Step 2. Compare/Contrast your own rating to those of your classmate and the entire class. Be sure to give examples of your activities to support your answer.

Test Section 2 B.1   The Best Shows on TV   *Option 1*

Step 1. Indicate the ways in which you and your classmates completed the sentence you were assigned.

1. The best TV shows do not present woman as _____.

2. The best TV shows do not present men as _____.

3. The best TV shows do not present children as _____.

4. The best TV shows do not present Jewish people as _____.

5. The best TV shows do not present people of African descent as
    _____.

6. The best TV shows do not present gays and lesbians as _____.

7. The best TV shows do not present _____ as _____.

Step 2. Now select one other sentence from Step 1 and complete it with information provided in the class discussion.

Step 3. Provide examples of TV programs, past and present, that fit the descriptions you have written. Come up with three programs in each category (for a total of six).

Grading the Responses

Option 1

Not only should we test what and how we teach, we should also grade, score, evaluate, and provide feedback consistent with what and how we teach. Now that we have test sections consistent with the what and how of teaching, we consider grading the responses. As has been emphasized and reiterated throughout this book, the core instructional event centers on communication. The learners have given information to each other, gathered it from each other, compared, contrasted, and evaluated it. They have drawn profiles, reached conclusions, and otherwise engaged in negotiating meaning. To create a testing event that parallels the instructional event requires that communication be the core of the testing event. Each of the test sections requires learners to communicate information gathered and exchanged during the instructional event. Table 8.1 illustrates one of the connections between instructional and testing events. Specifically, each step of the two test sections has been analyzed according to the in-class dynamic used to generate the test items.

Since the test sections focus on information and content, the scoring criteria ought to reflect this. For convenience of discussion and ease of mathematical calculation, each test section will be assigned 10 points. Ten is an arbitrary number; it could have been 20. One suggestion for grading the responses is to assign all 10 points for accuracy of information conveyed as shown in Table 8.2. The points can be evenly distributed among the various steps of the test section so that in Test Section 1 A.1, Steps 1 and 2 are each worth 5 points. Since Test Section 2 B.1 has three steps, 10 points cannot be evenly distributed; we therefore suggest that Step 1 be allotted 4 points and Steps 2 and 3 be allotted 3 points each, for a total of 10.

Option 2

In Chapter 7, task-based activities were shown to be the building blocks for providing other aspects of language instruction. The past tense, nominal forms of verbs, and word order in questions could be taught in conjunction with Activity A.1 What Did You Do Last Week? What follows, then, is a test section for Activity A.1 in which the direction lines and point distribution also reflect having used the activities as building blocks for other aspects of language instruction. We have maintained the point value of the test section at 10 only for reasons of drawing a parallel example. With the addition of

TABLE 8.1. Type of In-Class Interaction from which Test Information Is Drawn

	Test Section 1 A.1	Test Section 2 B.1
Step 1	group	group/class
Step 2	class	class
Step 3	—	class

TABLE 8.2. Point Distributions on Test Sections

	Test Section 1 A.1	Test Section 2 B.1
Step 1	5 points	4 points
Step 2	5 points	3 points
Step 3	—	3 points

linguistic structure and communication strategies to the grading criteria, it would make sense to add points to the value of the test section: Rather than maintain the value of the test section at 10, it would be reasonable and justifiable to raise it to 15.

Test Section 3 A.1   What Did You Do Last Week?   *Option 2*

Step 1. Compare/Contrast the rating you assigned to the classmate you interviewed with the rating we derived for the entire class. Be sure you give examples of his/her activities to support your answer. You will be graded for accuracy of information as well as for accuracy of past tense use and forms. (5 points total: 3 for information, 2 for past tense)
Step 2. Compare/Contrast your own rating with those of your classmate and the entire class. Be sure to give examples of your activities to support your answer. (5 points total: 3 for information, 2 for past tense. *Alternative:* 2 for use of communication strategies to mark comparison/contrast)

ISSUES SURROUNDING THIS APPROACH TO TESTING

Swaffar, Arens, and Byrnes (1991) included a section in their book in which they address questions surrounding their approach to the instruction of second language reading. These questions were asked by colleagues and by audience members who had attended their presentations. We offer a similar section that provides answers to frequently asked questions about our approach to testing.

Face Validity

One of the four criteria Carroll (1980) identified as characteristics of a good test was *acceptability.* The term takes the learners' point of view into consideration. It implies learners' willingness to participate in the testing and their satisfaction that the test evaluates their progress. "For many learners, acceptability is tied to familiarity. If they are not familiar with a testing format or procedure, they may view it as unacceptable. For example, if free spontaneous recall ('Write down everything that you remember reading without looking back at the passage') was not an activity type used in class, then the learners might not accept it as a valid way to test their reading comprehension. Likewise, if an instructor uses the target language only fifty percent of the time in class, the learners might not accept a test of listening comprehension" (Lee and VanPatten 1995, p. 135). Familiarity and face validity are related concepts. A test has *face validity* if it appears to be acceptable. Any test in any subject matter has face validity, and consequently is acceptable, if the content of the test and the content of the class are the same.

Memory

Successful test performance requires that learners memorize the content of in-class interactions. How are language learners supposed to remember what takes place in class?

Since the early days of language instruction, when tutors were hired to instruct the children of wealthy parents and when Latin was part of every curriculum, memory and memorization have played essential roles in language learning. For centuries, language learners memorized Latin declensions and Romance verb conjugations: regular verbs, irregular verbs, present, past, future, perfect, and conditional tenses, indicative and subjunctive moods. Memorization was a key component in Audiolingual Methodology. Many contemporary language instructors can recite at least one dialogue they memorized when they were enrolled in their introductory, first-term language class. The approach to language testing proposed here simply directs memory and memorization toward a different element of the instructional event.

Can learners recall the content and information generated from an activity? The results of the experiment presented in Chapter 4 clearly provide an affirmative response to the question. Memory for the content of the activity was very good immediately after the task-based activity was carried out. Recall of information was subcategorized by the three phases of the activity, and almost all of the learners recalled information from the three phases. One week later, these results still held. The learners had no idea that they would be asked to do another recall; during that week, they most certainly did not study for this second round of testing. So, without engaging in any out-of-class learning behaviors, they recalled the content. This evidence is the strongest that memory is not a large issue surrounding this approach to testing.

Collaboration

Successful test performance requires individual test-takers to rely on what they extracted from a group activity. In other words, individual's performances are not based solely on their own talents, intellect, or study habits. Is it fair to individuals to hold them accountable for the contributions that others make to an interaction?

When language is placed in communicative contexts, it is always discussed in terms of a collaboration between speakers and hearers or readers and writers (Kramsch 1993; Swaffar et al. 1991). Grice (1975) formulated maxims that govern the cooperation between speaker and hearer in ordinary conversations. Even the words *conversation* and *dialogue* are defined in terms of exchanges between multiple participants. It seems natural, then, to extend notions of cooperation and exchange to instructional settings, in particular to testing events, since language use is collaborative.

Outside of language departments, collaborative-based learning, teaching, and testing is found in abundance. Business schools, science curricula, and engineering departments assign students to work in research teams, management groups, or work teams. The teams are given a project to carry out, a problem to solve, or a machine to design. All members of the group are held accountable for the product that results from their interaction. Their collaboration is evaluated based on how well the project was executed, the solution(s) offered to the problem, or the design developed for the machine. The rationale for these collaborative undertakings in the academic setting is the nature of nonacademic settings. In the latter, teams often must work closely on assignments. Since the nonacademic world works collaboratively, the academic world encourages, provides opportunities for, and evaluates collaborative efforts. Language, in both academic and nonacademic contexts, is based on collaboration. And so we reiterate a previous point: It seems natural to create collaboratively based testing events.

Target Language Versus Native Language

All the activities and test sections in this book are presented in English. But what if you are teaching Italian or Portuguese? Should you write the direction lines in English or in Italian or Portuguese?

The research that has examined the effects of requiring target language versus native language responses to reading tests has provided very clear and definitive results. Beginning-level language learners, undergraduate language majors, and Israeli high school students taking an English language test for admittance to a university all performed significantly better when allowed to respond to items in their native language or items written in their native language (Lee 1986, 1987; Shohamy 1984; Wolf 1993b). The implication for those conducting reading research is to assess comprehension via the native language (Bernhardt 1992; Wolf 1993a). Learners may well have comprehended what they read, but may not be able to express, relate, or otherwise indicate their level of comprehension due to limited second language production abilities.

But as Wolf (1993a) points out, the curricular implications are not quite so clear. Certainly, native language direction lines and responses to reading are desirable in order to maximize the learners' expression of their comprehension. Yet for curricula in which the second language is used from the first day of instruction, other factors may sway the decision to use or not use the native language in direction lines and responses.

The activities and test sections presented in this book are not about reading in a second language, but rather speaking and interacting via the target language. At the very least, the test sections should require target language use, since the interactions on which they are based required target language use. The direction lines present other issues. First, you do not want the directions to be incomprehensible. Learners may well have the information and language necessary to respond to the item, but they cannot do so unless they understand the directions. The suggestion is, then, to provide learners direction lines in their native language during the first year of instruction, but transition to the target language in the second year and beyond. In the first year, learners should be given general directions that tell them to respond in the target language unless otherwise noted.

Specificity of Direction Lines

In his seminal work on language testing, Bachman (1990) indicates that test-takers' perceptions of the test and hence their performance can be expected to be affected by how they are instructed to respond, because they will adopt differing response strategies accordingly (p. 120). Performance depends to a great extent on the degree to which test-takers understand the procedures to be followed, the nature of the task they are to complete, and the specification of the task via direction lines.

The following example illustrates the point. In Lee (1995), a task-based activity that examined stereotypes was developed. That activity was used as the basis for developing the types of test sections presented in this chapter. The first version of that test section was worded as follows.

> **Version 1.** In a paragraph, indicate to what extent you personally agree or disagree with the class's choice [of the three most stereotypical characterizations].

A person attending the conference at which these ideas were presented commented that indicating agreement or disagreement in and of itself did not require a paragraph. Agreement could be indicated in a sentence, and so she feared that, given the direction lines, a number of her students would write no more than a sentence. We then added another sentence.

> **Version 2.** In a paragraph, indicate to what extent you personally agree or disagree with the class's choice [of the three most stereotypical characterizations]. Explain your answer.

A person attending the conference at which this second version was presented suggested that "explain your answer" might be a more appropriate direction line for higher-level learners than for beginners. She suggested that from a communicative perspective, it would be easier both linguistically and cognitively, as well as more affectively positive, for first-year learners to provide examples than it would be for them to explain an answer. She provided an excellent suggestion; the most appropriate formulation of the direction line for beginning-level learners follows.

> **Version 3.** In a paragraph, indicate to what extent you personally agree or disagree with your group's selection and with the class's

selection [of the three most stereotypical characterizations]. You must give examples of specific movies, magazines, books, or popular conceptions that support your answer.

Indeed, providing specific examples constitutes a satisfactory explanation for beginning language learners.

At Higher Levels

In Chapter 6, two versions of Activity A were developed for use at higher levels of instruction. What are appropriate test sections for these higher levels?

The activities generated for these levels of instruction followed from the application of the following criteria.

a. Increase the information load.
b. Explore more subtopics or more complex subtopics.
c. Alter the way in which linguistic support is provided.

The test sections developed from these activities also reflect these criteria. The following test sections were developed from Activities A.2 and A.3, respectively. Since they are directed toward higher levels of instruction, the direction lines would be presented in the language of study, not in the learners' native language.

Test Section 4 A.2   More Physically or More Mentally Active?

Step 1. Indicate the name of the person you interviewed: _____ First, indicate what type of week he/she had, giving examples of his/her activities to support your evaluation.

MENTAL ACTIVITY			PHYSICAL ACTIVITY		
VERY	SOMEWHAT	NOT AT ALL	VERY	SOMEWHAT	NOT AT ALL
1	2 3	4 5	1	2 3	4 5

Step 2. Compare/Contrast your partner's week with the class's and with your own.

Test Section 5 A.3   Mentally and Physically Active

Step 1. Indicate which of the following statements the class selected as true.
    a. It is easier to add mental activity to a physical one.
    b. It is easier to add physical activity to a mental one.
    c. It is just as easy to add mental activity to a physical one as it is to add physical activity to a mental one.
Step 2. Provide examples of activities that the class used to justify its conclusion.
Step 3. Come up with at least two original examples (not discussed in class) that either (a) support the conclusion or (b) contradict the conclusion.

Acceptability of New Ideas

The following quote describes a graduate teaching assistant's response to an affectively negative testing event. (The test was much too long for the time allotted.) The teaching assistant was teaching for the first time and was teaching in a multisection course.

"[The instructor] was unable to make the connection between the way she was teaching and all parts of the exam. She felt that the exam as a whole did not reflect the way she had been shown (by me) to teach the course. She came to me and said that, as an instructor, she felt frustrated and that her students, too, felt frustrated by the exam. As we talked, I reassured her about her teaching methodology, and then we went over the exam section by section. Several realizations emerged from our talk. I recognized that some sections were not as effective as they could have been, and she saw the reasoning behind other sections. We both realized that her students probably did not understand *how* she was covering the material; she was so natural about using the language and creating interesting activities that the "lesson" part of classroom interactions (that is, what students should learn) had escaped her students' attention. [The instructor] was given the task of writing two sections for the next exam. She was to come up with formats that she felt reflected what she was doing. She also decided to be more explicit with students about what material needed to be studied and about how she was covering the material" (Lee 1989, p. 75).

The following are among the many lessons to be learned from this example.

- Instructional innovation needs to be supported by testing innovation.
- Communication (i.e., natural language use) may sometimes mask other elements of language instruction.
- Information about what and how language learners are learning must be made explicit to them.

To use Carroll's often quoted principle of language testing (c.f., Krashen & Terrell 1983; Lee & VanPatten 1995; Shrum & Glisan 1994), the above example demonstrates the principle of acceptability. Neither the instructor nor her class of learners found the test acceptable. For a test to be effective, it must be acceptable to the test-takers (and to the test-givers!).

Given all these considerations, we offer the following suggestions to aid instructors in presenting this approach to testing to their learners, as well as to aid learners and instructors in accepting this approach to testing.

1. Create a new section for the test in addition to more traditional test sections.
2. Label the section Classroom Activities.
3. Provide options within the section.
4. Provide learners a study guide that lists the classroom activities from which you will select test items.
5. Weight the test section appropriately.

Once instructors accept and implement "new" ideas, they are well advised to communicate to learners some background surrounding these innovations. Providing select (not complete) information regarding the *what*, the *how*, and the *why* of an innovation may help learners accept it.

The first suggestion is to combine this new test section with sections that are more traditional and hence acceptable to learners. In addition to being tested on the content of in-class interactions, learners are also tested in areas such as vocabulary, grammar, reading, etc. The testing event, then, is a blend of old and new. It would seem drastic to present learners with a chapter or unit test or a midterm exam that contained only test sections such as those presented in this book. Once they become accustomed to this type of testing, they might find a test based exclusively on in-class activities far more acceptable.

The test section should be labeled so as to identify for the test-takers the source of information they need to access in order to perform successfully on this section of the test. Classroom Activities or In-Class Exchanges are two labels that achieve this goal. An important issue surrounding this approach to testing is class attendance. For whatever reasons, few learners manage to attend each and every class. One way to allow for absenteeism is to give learners options within the test section. They could, for example, be directed to complete two of five items.

The suggestion to provide learners a list of classroom activities from which an instructor will choose the exam section also addresses the issue of acceptability. Such a list allows learners to focus their study efforts. Many instructors resist this suggestion because they feel they are giving something away, but that really isn't the case. Consider the test for a driver's license. We all know exactly what will take place during a driving test. We know we have to parallel park, back up several hundred feet, and respond to traffic signals. In short, we know what they will test and how they will do it. This knowledge does not, however, guarantee that everyone passes the test, but does focus student-drivers' learning efforts. The parallel with language instruction is that providing a list of activities to the learners provides them the knowledge of what will be tested and how. Even though they can focus their learning, not everyone will do equally well on the test.

Finally, the classroom activities portion of the exam must be weighted appropriately. Shrum and Glisan maintain that "if students spend 50% of their class time developing oral skills, then nearly half of their test should evaluate their oral skills" (1994, p. 227). Extending this principle to other class-time endeavors, we would expect the total point distribution on a test to reflect a balance between the various learning activities that take place in and out of the language classroom.

PRIVILEGING THE MENTAL PROCESSES UNDERLYING TASK-BASED ACTIVITIES

Many instructors resist the idea of testing the specific content generated during in-class exchanges because of absenteeism. They do not want to confound learners' test performance with their class attendance. No matter the merits of this argument, there are other means for underscoring the importance of in-class interaction. Specifically, test sections can reflect the mental processes involved in carrying out the task-based activities. These sections engage the test-takers in the same type of cognitive activity (selecting, categorizing, evaluating, concluding, etc.) that in-class activities require. As a result of attending class and participating in the instructional events, learners should be more successful on the test sections. The following two test sections have been derived from Activities A.1 and B.1. Each test section privileges the mental processes involved carrying out its companion task-based in-class activity and is formulated such that a learner who was absent the day the activity was carried out could still complete the test section.

Test Section 6 A.1 What Did You Do Last Week? *Mental Processes*

Step 1. Make a list of ten things you did last week. Five of them must be sedentary and the other five must be physically active. (5 points total: 3 for information, 2 for past tense)

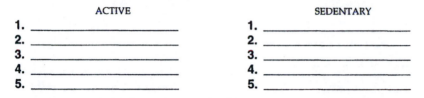

	ACTIVE		SEDENTARY
1.	_____	1.	_____
2.	_____	2.	_____
3.	_____	3.	_____
4.	_____	4.	_____
5.	_____	5.	_____

Step 2. Use the following rating scale to assess your level of physical activity. Be sure to give examples of your activities to support your answer. (5 points total: 3 for information, 2 for past tense. *Alternative:* 2 for use of communication strategies to mark comparison/contrast)

VERY SEDENTARY		AS SEDENTARY AS ACTIVE		VERY ACTIVE
1	2	3	4	5

Test Section 7 B.1 The Best Shows on TV *Mental Processes*

Step 1. Complete three of the following sentences with at least two pieces of true information. (5 points total: 3 points for information, 2 points for correct syntax)

1. The best TV shows do not present women as _____ .
2. The best TV shows do not present men as _____ .
3. The best TV shows do not present children as _____ .
4. The best TV shows do not present Jewish people as _____ .
5. The best TV shows do not present people of African descent as

    _____ .

6. The best TV shows do not present gays and lesbians as _____ .
7. The best TV shows do not present _____ as _____ .

Step 2. Provide examples of TV programs, past and present, that fit the descriptions you have written. Come up with 2 programs in each category (for a total of six). (5 points total: 3 for information, 2 for use of communication strategies for providing examples)

An Option

The original classroom activities required learners to gather information from each other and then somehow to assess this information. The two test sections that privilege the mental processes involved in the classroom activities have learners providing their own information and then assessing it. An option available to test developers is to provide some information in the first part of the test section that the test-takers must then evaluate, assess, and come to conclusions about. The parallel to the class format is obvious: Test-takers work with information supplied to them just as learners work with information they gather. Test Section 8 A.1 is just such a parallel to Activity A.1.

Test Section 8 A.1   What Did You Do Last Week?   *Mental Processes* (option)

Step 1. Read over the list of activities your instructor did last week. Indicate if each activity is sedentary or physically active. (2 points total)

		ACTIVE	SEDENTARY
1.	I danced at a party for 3 hours.	❑	❑
2.	I played tennis a couple of times.	❑	❑
3.	I researched a paper.	❑	❑
4.	I graded quizzes.	❑	❑
5.	I held office hours.	❑	❑
6.	I walked to work those two days that we had that wonderful weather.	❑	❑
7.	I wrote a few letters.	❑	❑
8.	I went shopping.	❑	❑
9.	I spent all day Saturday cleaning house and doing laundry.	❑	❑
10.	I watched the Thursday night line-up on TV.	❑	❑

Step 2. Use the following rating scale to assess your instructor's level of physical activity. Be sure to give examples of your own activities to support your answer. (3 points total)

VERY SEDENTARY	AS SEDENTARY AS ACTIVE	VERY ACTIVE
1 2	3	4 5

Step 3. Compare and contrast your instructor's level of physical activity with your own. (5 points total: 2 for information, 1 for past tense, 2 for use of communication strategies to mark comparison/contrast)

SUMMARY

No discussion of teaching is really complete without a concomitant consideration of testing. The first seven chapters of this book present a task-based framework for engaging in communicative language teaching. The present chapter is the first of two that consider task-based testing. Tests are useful instruments for shaping behavior, both instructors' as well as learners.' As Shohamy (1993) documents, behaviors can change even at the national level. Instructors might select particular content and emphasize particular materials. Learners might shape their in-class behaviors according to testing expectations. Hopefully the tests would shape, in a positive way, their out-of-class learning behaviors.

Two types of classroom tests were presented. The first examined the specific content of in-class interactions. For example, Activity A.1 requires the class to draw a profile of itself according to the types of activities they engaged in the week before. The profile they draw becomes the focus of the test items. Test-takers first have to recount the details of the profile and then provide a personal perspective on it. The second type of test incorporated items that reflect the mental processes learners used to complete the in-class activities, but did not examine specific information that emerged in class. For example, if learners draw a profile in class, the test also has them draw a profile but not recount the details of the profile drawn in class. The issues surrounding this approach to testing are many, including students' capacity to remember what happens in class, direction lines, and the acceptability of new ideas. These issues are not insurmountable, and suggestions were offered to address them.

To say that something is *coherent* is to say that it is marked by an orderly or logical relation of parts that affords comprehension or recognition. To the extent that teaching and testing are an entwined enterprise, they should be marked by a logical relation of parts. We have attempted to provide a coherent picture of teaching and testing by deriving test sections from the activities presented in earlier chapters. In the following chapter, the discussion of testing moves into the domain of oral testing.

GAINING GREATER PERSPECTIVE

1. *Power of Tests.* Shohamy's 1993 essay is a case study, albeit at the national level, that parallels events in the United States. Hers is a cautionary tale regarding the uses and potential abuses of standardized tests.
2. *Ideas for Testing.* Lee and VanPatten (1995), Shrum and Glisan (1994), and Omaggio Hadley (1993) all offer chapters on classroom testing. The most complete treatment, the one that is integrated throughout this book, is that of Lee and VanPatten.

APPLICATION ACTIVITIES

1. Test sections that privilege the specific content of in-class interactions were developed for Activities A.1 and B.1. Now develop test sections for the following.
   a. Activities A.2 and A.3 (Chapter 6)
   b. Activity Bilingualism and Biculturalism (Chapter 4)
   c. The higher-level versions of Activity B.1 (if you developed them as part of the Application Activities in Chapter 6)

2. Application Activities 5 and 6 in Chapter 7 asked you to develop grammar notes for the following. Take these versions of the activities and develop test sections that assign points to use of the grammar.
   a. Activity A.3 (Chapter 6)
   b. Activity Bilingualism and Biculturalism (Chapter 4)
   c. The higher-level versions of Activity B.1 (if you developed them as part of the Application Activities in Chapter 6)
3. Test sections that privilege the mental processes of in-class interactions were developed for Activities A.1 and B.1. Now develop similar test sections for the following. Try to identify rhetorical organizational devices that would be appropriate to grade for.
   a. Activities A.2 and A.3 (Chapter 6)
   b. Activity Bilingualism and Biculturalism (Chapter 4)
   c. The higher-level versions of Activity B.1 (if you developed them as part of the Application Activities in Chapter 6)
4. The following activity was presented in the Application Activities that accompanied Chapter 5. Take this activity and develop two test sections, one that privileges the specific content of the in-class interaction and another that privileges the mental processes involved.

Activity. How Do You React?

Step 1. What do you think about the idea of eating or drinking the following foods? Use the scale to indicate your reaction.

YES, I WOULD LIKE TO TRY IT.		YES, BUT ONLY A LITTLE.		ONLY IF IT WERE ABSOLUTELY NECESSARY.
1	2	3	4	5

1. _____ a glass of camel's milk
2. _____ a cup of coffee with camel's milk
3. _____ meat preserved via radiation treatment
4. _____ meat preserved via radiation treatment after it was stored for 8 years
5. _____ seaweed salad
6. _____ seaweed soup
7. _____ fruit preserved via radiation treatment
8. _____ fruit heavily treated with pesticides
9. _____ monkey brains
10. _____ roe (fish eggs: caviar)

Step 2. Compare your reactions to those of one or two classmates. Do you agree on your preferences?

Step 3. Compare your reactions to those of the rest of the class. What foods does the majority want to try? What foods would the majority try only if it were absolutely necessary?

Step 4. Which statement best describes the class?
   a. Eating is an adventure and we are adventurers.
   b. We are somewhat conservative in our tastes.
   c. We would eat anything if we had to.

    d. We would rather die than try certain foods.

    e. Other: _____

5. A concern in multisection courses is that each instructor grade the same way. We refer to this desired outcome as *interrater reliability*. Test Sections 6 A.1 and 7 B.1 appear to elicit rather individualized responses from learners. Suggest some guidelines to give instructors of multisection courses to correct Test Sections 6 and 7 so that each learner, no matter the instructor, is graded in a similar way.

CHAPTER 9

Task-Based Oral Testing

CHAPTER OVERVIEW

In Chapter 8 we made the link between in-class interactions and in-class or written tests. In this chapter we link instructional practices and oral testing. Test formats are developed that have one test-taker and one test-giver, as well as formats that involve multiple test-takers. In addition to discussing issues surrounding this approach to oral testing, suggestions are offered for scoring learner performance via a multicomponential scale. Finally, we present the transcripts of two groups of learners taking an oral test. One group was enrolled in first-semester Spanish and the other was enrolled in fourth-semester Spanish. A comparison and contrast is made between the two groups.

ORAL TESTS DERIVED FROM TASK-BASED ACTIVITIES

Lee and VanPatten (1995) describe, compare, and contrast two tests of oral proficiency, the Oral Proficiency Interview (OPI) and the Israeli National Oral Proficiency Test (INOPT). Both tests present advantages and disadvantages for examining the communicative language ability of a test-taker. These proficiency exams are not, however, tied or connected in any way to classroom practices. By virtue of being proficiency measures, they are supposed to measure ability independent of the instructional means by which learners have developed communicative language ability. In contrast, the oral tests developed for this section of the chapter have been created with reference to very particular instructional events. Even though the two oral tests reflect the principle of testing what and how you teach, they require distinctly different interactional patterns. The first parallels the pattern of the OPI in that there are only two parties involved, a test-taker and a test-giver. The second parallels the interactional pattern of in-class task-based activities in that the oral exchange involves multiple test-takers who carry out a task-based activity.

Among the differences between being the sole test-taker and one of many test-takers is the communicative burden each individual carries. *Communicative burden* refers to "the responsibility of an individual test-taker to initiate, respond, manage, and negotiate an oral event" (Lee & VanPatten 1995, p. 179). Multiple participants each take on a communicative burden; each must initiate, respond, manage, and negotiate the oral event. The sole test-taker, by way of contrast, is the one who carries almost all of the communicative burden.

An oral test derived from in-class activities should certainly meet the criterion of being acceptable to the test-takers, since they will be familiar with the format as well as the requirements of the task. All in all, linking the oral test to classroom activities may well motivate learners' participation, since such participation is the best type of learning behavior for being successful during the testing event.

One Test-Taker and One Test-Giver

Oral testing is usually carried out as an interaction between two people, an individual test-taker and an individual test-giver. It is the most labor- and time-intensive approach to oral testing. The OPI and the oral interview segment of the INOPT utilize a question-and-answer format as the basis of the interview. By linking the content of the oral test with the content of an instructional event, the test-taker/test-giver interaction is less interview and more reporting. The test-giver participates actively in the oral testing event not only by virtue of his or her physical presence but by the prompt questions he or she asks in order to manage the event. The test-giver can take on a different role in the oral testing event by co-constructing content. That is, the test-taker and the test-giver can carry out a task-based activity as if they were partners assigned to work together. Both the report/interview and the test-giver-as-partner formats are exemplified below.

Reporting Content

The multiphase approach used in the OPI, INOPT, and here for structuring the report/interview was adapted originally from the Foreign Service Institute's oral test (Lowe 1982). Since the content of the interview is a report of an in-class activity, the format runs the risk of having the test-taker report information the test-giver already knows (assuming the test-giver is the test-taker's instructor). Following Lee and VanPatten (1995, p. 182), the last phase of the test is called "Beyond the Activity" and provides for the exchange of new information between the test-giver and test-taker. The test-taker's report of the activity in Phase 3 sets up this communicative exchange. This type of oral test is exemplified in Oral Test Section 9 A.1   What Did You Do Last Week?—Reporting. (Test sections for higher-level activities are presented in a subsequent section.)

Oral Test Section 9 A.1   What Did You Do Last Week?   *Reporting*

Phase 1. *Warm up.* Make the test-taker feel comfortable.
Phase 2. *Initial questioning.* Who did you work with on this activity? Have you worked with these people before? Was it a good grouping?

Phase 3. *Activity-related questions.* What kind of activities did you classify as active? Which ones did you classify as sedentary? What did you add to the list? What kind of week did the class have? What kind of week did the classmate you interviewed have? Which examples support your evaluation?

Phase 4. *Beyond the activity.* What about your own week? Do you fit the class profile? Give examples of specific activities that you engaged in to support your answer.

Test-Giver as Partner

The test-giver is a participant in the testing event by virtue of his or her presence and their role as prompter and questioner. The test-giver asks questions and the test-taker responds. In Chapter 2, we questioned the *communication = question & answer* paradigm in the classroom and proposed task-based activities as a means of incorporating other dimensions of communication into the classroom. The testing event can be structured as a task-based activity resulting in a testing event that is truly communicative from its outset, as shown in Oral Test Section 10 A.1.

Oral Test Section 10 A.1   What Did You Do Last Week?   *Test-Giver as Partner*

Step 1. Working together, you (the test-taker) and your partner (the test-giver) indicate whether each activity is active or sedentary.

	SEDENTARY	ACTIVE
1. dancing at a party	❑	❑
2. riding a bike	❑	❑
3. playing video games	❑	❑
4. playing a sport	❑	❑
5. reading a book	❑	❑
6. watching TV	❑	❑
7. writing a letter	❑	❑
8. making dinner	❑	❑

Step 2. Add three activities to the list, preferably three that you or your partner engage in, and indicate whether they are active or sedentary.

	SEDENTARY	ACTIVE
_____	❑	❑
_____	❑	❑
_____	❑	❑

Step 3. Interview the test-giver about what he or she did last week. Keep track of the answers, since you will need them in Step 4.

Step 4. Use the following scale to rate your partner's week.

VERY SEDENTARY		AS SEDENTARY AS ACTIVE		VERY ACTIVE
1	2	3	4	5

Present the rating to your partner and find out if he or she agrees with the rating.

Multiple Test-Takers

The INOPT includes among its four formats a group discussion. As Shohamy, Reves, and Bejerano (1986) point out, performance on an oral interview requires a different speech style than do group discussions, reporting content, or role plays. Four test-takers participate in the group discussion but the test-giver does not. The test-giver remains a silent observer whose function is to evaluate the performance of each test-taker individually. Even though the four form a group, each individual is graded separately. It should be easy, then, to picture a group interaction constructed around a task-based activity. Oral Test Section 11 B.1 is adapted from the in-class version of Activity B.1   The Best Shows on TV.

Oral Test Section 11 B.1   The Best Shows on TV   *Multiple Participants*

Step 1. As a group, select three of the following sentences and complete them with at least three different pieces of information.
1. The best TV shows do not present women as _____ .
2. The best TV shows do not present men as _____ .
3. The best TV shows do not present children as _____ .
4. The best TV shows do not present Jewish people as _____ .
5. The best TV shows do not present people of African descent as

   _____ .
6. The best TV shows do not present gays and lesbians as _____ .
7. The best TV shows to not present _____ as _____ .

Step 2. Now that you have characterized the treatment of people on the best shows on TV, identify programs, past and present, that fit your descriptions.
Step 3. Propose a new show that would have characters from each of the groups of people you worked with in Step 1.

ISSUES SURROUNDING TASK-BASED ORAL TESTING

Bias or Neutrality

Many hail multiple-choice machine-scored tests as objective measures of performance in contrast to essay-based tests, which are said to be more subjective measures. You cannot test oral language via a multiple-choice machine-scored test. Nor can you test oral language via a written essay. How can oral tests that require person-to-person ongoing interaction be as objective as possible?

Two issues present themselves when the test-taker and test-giver have a preexisting relationship. The nature of the relationship may be personal or professional, as in the case of the test-taker being enrolled in the test-giver's class. One of the issues is *bias* or *neutrality*. Given a preexisting relationship, the test-giver may have preformed notions and expectations, positive or negative, of the test-taker's abilities. If a test-giver allows these preformed notions to influence the evaluation of a specific testing event, such as the oral test, the evaluation is biased in a certain direction. Such test-givers are not acting as neutral parties. Each testing event should be free of bias and characterized by neutrality. Learners' previous test scores, absenteeism, attitude in class, or personality should not register in the oral testing event.

Another issue surrounding oral testing as it has been presented here is that of having test-takers display shared knowledge. Is there real communication taking place if both test-taker and test-giver were participants in the event being reported? Having a test-giver ask, for example, "What were the three characteristics the class came up with?" seems communicatively artificial since the test-giver not only was present for the instructional event, but also managed the in-class interaction. The test-giver knows what the three characteristics were; he or she was there!

Mary Wildner Bassett (Department of German at the University of Arizona) and L. Kathy Heilenman (Department of French and Italian at the University of Iowa) have implemented procedures that address both bias and displaying shared knowledge. Quite simply, they require that language learners take oral tests with someone other than their own instructor. In one case, different instructors are assigned to examine entire classes. In the other, learners sign up for a time to be tested, and a test-giver is then assigned to that time slot. This procedure allows the testing event to be a true communicative exchange in that the test-giver would not have participated in the instructional event the learner is reporting. In both cases, test-givers and test-takers are unknown to each other. They have no existing relationship that might bias the evaluation, and any questions the test-giver would ask about an instructional event are real questions. The test-giver did not participate in the instructional event from which the test is derived.

Preparing for the Oral Test

As previously noted, Krashen and Terrell (1983) look for tests that support in-class activities. They want the learners to engage in good learning behaviors outside of class in order to prepare for the tests. What steps can be taken to have language learners use the language outside of class as a means to prepare for the oral test?

In the previous chapter, the issue of acceptability of new ideas was addressed and several suggestions were offered that help learners accept an innovation in testing format. Two of those suggestions can be used to help learners prepare for the oral test.

1. Provide options within the test section.
2. Provide learners a study guide that lists the classroom activities from which you will select test items.

For the oral test, the test-giver can prepare a set of index cards on which are written the names of in-class activities. The cards could be spread out on a desk, face down. The test-taker could then select two cards, read them, and hand the card of choice to the test-giver. The oral test would then proceed. Chances should be small that the learner was absent the days both activities were performed. The test-giver could also provide learners a list of the activities from which they will be selecting one. The benefit is that suggested by Krashen and Terrell (1983): In order to prepare for the test, learners will be engaged in good learning behaviors. The best way to prepare for the oral test is to meet with other learners outside of class and carry out the activities together.

Appropriate Scoring Criteria

Defining *communication* as the expression, interpretation, and negotiation of meaning recognizes various processes involved when two or more people come together. The Canale and Swain (1980) model of communicative competence is built from four component competencies: sociolinguistic, discourse, strategic, and grammatical competence. Given the componential perspective taken on communication, what are appropriate componential scoring criteria?

Bachman and Palmer (1983) created componential rating scales using three categories: grammatical competence, pragmatic (discourse) competence, and sociolinguistic competence. Within the category of pragmatic competence, they identify and describe two component competencies: vocabulary and cohesion. The descriptions of cohesion, for example, identify five levels to distinguish learner performance. They are the following.

1. Utterances completely disjointed, or discourse too short to judge.
2. Relationships between utterances not adequately marked; frequent confusing relationships among ideas.
3. Relationship between utterances generally marked; sometimes confusing relationships among ideas.
4. Relationships between utterances well marked.
5. Uses a variety of appropriate devices; hardly ever confusing relationships among ideas.

Within the category of sociolinguistic competence, they identify and describe three component competencies: distinguishing of registers, nativeness (accuracy), and use of cultural references. Furthermore, they assign different point values to each of the competencies, indicating their relative importance to the evaluation of learner performance. Table 9.1 presents the point distribution and ranges for each competence.

> **Consider how much class time is devoted to oral language use and development. If half the class time is oriented toward oral language, should half the test points be accounted for by oral language use? In a communicatively oriented course and curriculum, what percentage of the final course grade should be derived from scores on oral tests or oral sections of tests?**

TABLE 9.1. Point Distribution of Bachman and Palmer Componential Rating Scales

Competence	Rating Scale						
Grammatical	0	1	2	3	4	5	6
Pragmatic							
Vocabulary	0	1	2	3	4		
Cohesion	0	1	2	3	4		
Sociolinguistic							
Registers	0	1	2	3.5			
Nativeness		1		3	4		
Cultural references	0.5		2.5	4			

TABLE 9.2. Componential Rating Scale for Content/Information Conveyed

Points	Descriptors
2	Minimal information; information lacks substance, is superficial; inappropriate or irrelevant information; or not enough information to evaluate
4	Limited information; ideas present but not developed; lack of supporting detail or evidence
6	Adequate information; some development of ideas; some ideas lack supporting detail or evidence
8	Very complete information; no more can be said; thorough; relevant; on target

Source: Adapted from Lee et al. 1996, p. A19.

Clearly, the Bachman and Palmer componential rating scales account for a wide variety of components of communicative language ability. Lee and Van-Patten suggest adapting the Bachman and Palmer scales, or any other scales, for use in particular instructional contexts by altering the weight of a scale and/or varying the components. If course materials emphasize pragmatic competence via explicit instruction in communication and organization strategies, the points assigned to cohesion are increased. Given that the approach to both classroom and oral testing has emphasized the connection to classroom interaction, an additional component that ought to be evaluated on oral tests derived from task-based activities is that of content or information conveyed. The scale shown in Table 9.2 serves as an example and guide for describing and evaluating learner performance in the area of content.

You may have noted that the points assigned to this component are greater than those assigned to any other component. This decision was made purposefully to reflect the emphasis, importance, and omnipresence of content in classroom interaction. The relative point value for the components should parallel the relative emphasis of that component in the instructional setting. In applying the principle of testing what and how we teach to oral testing, we must examine not only *how* learners say something—that is, cohesively and with accurate form—but also *what* they say, the content of their discourse.

Additionally, it is important to provide test-takers these criteria prior to the testing event. Knowledge of the criteria affects performance in that it shapes learners' behaviors, test-taking strategies, and attention. Two examples should underscore the point: One refers to learners' overall performance and the other to performance on a specific test section. Learners who are enrolled in a course on a Pass/Fail or Credit/No Credit basis tend to perform only to the level of passing or receiving credit. They constantly assess their involvement in the class, on homework, and for test preparation by asking themselves, What do I need to do to pass? More specifically, on a test section for which learners must write a paragraph on some topic, the criteria will shape their behaviors, focus their attention, and alter their test-taking strategies. If all the points allotted to the paragraph are for correct grammar, the learners know that the content does not matter. They can invent whatever they want as long as they use correct forms! If the points are allotted to content and to spelling, the learners would be attentive not only to what they say but also to spelling. Not knowing that spelling counts could affect test performance quite negatively. Whatever the criteria, the test-takers should be familiar with them and understand them.

Defining and Rewarding Appropriate Behavior

Collaboration is a key element in using task-based activities as the basis of classroom tests and oral tests. How, then, can learners be made aware of and rewarded for collaborative behaviors?

Shrum and Glisan (1994, pp. 318–319) provide Donato's (1992) system for monitoring and evaluating group speaking activities. The system requires the instructor to assess and record learner performance across four performance objectives. The scoring is based on a "+", "√", "–" system and then converted to points and grades. The performance objectives are provided in Table 9.3 You may note that the word TALK is an acronym for identifying the four performance objectives.

Although Donato's system may function well in primary and secondary instructional contexts, it might lack the specificity needed in post-secondary contexts. The following criteria for evaluating group interaction (Table 9.4) address appropriate adult learner behavior by defining acceptable and unacceptable interactional patterns. The parameters for evaluating individuals' performance during group interaction are four behaviors: domination, marginalization, support, and maintenance. These four behaviors are grouped into four categories, with each category given a different point value. The higher point value reflects the more valued, desired, and esteemed group interaction behaviors.

These criteria also could be used diagnostically to provide learners feedback during in-class group activities. Learners should be familiar not only with the task demands but also with the evaluation criteria prior to entering into a testing event. The wording of the four behaviors within the four categories should provide learners sufficient direction for reinforcing or correcting their behaviors. These same criteria then could be used to evaluate learner performance during the oral test in which multiple participants are examined simultaneously.

TABLE 9.3. Donato's System for Monitoring and Evaluating Group Speaking Activities

T = Talk	Is the learner talking? Is the learner trying to communicate? Is the talk task-relevant?
A = Accurate	Is the learner performing at an acceptable level of accuracy? Does the learner demonstrate the point of the lesson that is being used in the activity?
L = Listening	Is the learner on task? Does the learner listen to his or her partner or partners? Does the learner listen to directions?
K = Kind	Is the learner kind and cooperative? Does the learner kill the activity by his or her lack of cooperation? Does the learner work with his or her group?

TABLE 9.4. Criteria for Evaluating Group Interaction

Points	Behaviors
20	Does not dominate the interaction. Does not marginalize other participants. Provides verbal and nonverbal support to other participants. Is pivotal in maintaining the interaction and moving the other participants through the activity.
15	Sometimes takes over but does not dominate all phases of the activity. Sometimes marginalizes other participants. Tends to provide verbal and nonverbal support to other participants. Helps maintain the interaction and move the other participants through the activity.
10	Tends to dominate. Tends to marginalize other participants. Rarely offers verbal and nonverbal support to other participants. Rarely helps maintain the interaction and move the other participants through the activity.
5	Dominates the interaction so that few others can contribute. Marginalizes other participants. Does not offer verbal or nonverbal support to other participants. Does not help maintain the interaction and move the other participants through the activity.

Sample Procedures and a Sample Multicomponential Scale

The following procedures and evaluation criteria (Figure 9.1) are offered as examples of oral testing procedures and grading scales. Note that the procedures are directed to the test-takers themselves. In other words, instructors or test-givers infer their roles from what they know of the test-takers' roles. Note also

To the Students,

1. You will be examined as you interact, in Spanish, in groups of three or, if and when necessary, in groups of four.
2. The group will be given an activity to carry out. You should make an effort to carry out the activity in the time allotted. Note, however, that you will not be graded on whether you finish the steps, but on the type of information you contribute to the interaction. Obviously, the more steps you complete, the more opportunity you have to contribute. It is very important that you speak Spanish and work in Spanish with the other group members.
3. Procedures
   a. Each member of the group will be given a copy of the activity. (Different groups will be assigned different activities.) You may not write on this copy and you must return it to the instructor when your exam is finished.
   b. You will have 8 minutes (the time it takes the preceding group to interact) to read over the activity and think about the various steps involved as well as some possible ideas you might want to bring up. You will not be allowed to talk with other group members during this 8-minute preparation period, nor can you consult dictionaries or textbooks. You will not be able to use any notes you jot down during this preparation period.
   c. The group will come together to carry out the activity. The interaction will last for only 8 minutes. Your instructor will stop the activity after 8 minutes.
   d. At no time during the 8-minute interaction will the instructor/evaluator participate in the interaction. You may not ask the instructor/evaluator questions of any type. The instructor/evaluator will not interfere in the group dynamic under any circumstances.
4. Each member of the group will be evaluated separately. There will be no group grade assigned.
5. The evaluation criteria follow on the next pages. Please read them carefully, in particular the criteria that refer to group interaction. The point is not for you to talk more than the other group members but to help everyone in the group participate.

CRITERIA FOR EVALUATION   Name: _____

                          Total points: _____

CONTENT/INFORMATION CONVEYED

20–18 points
Contributes relevant information.
Develops ideas by speaking in multiple sentences.
Consistent performance across the entire activity.

17–16 points
Contributes relevant information.
Some development of ideas but tends to use single sentences.
Not-so-consistent performance across the entire activity.

15–14 points
Contributes adequate information.
Not much development of ideas.
Almost always speaks in single sentences.

FIGURE 9.1 Sample Oral Testing Procedures and Evaluation Criteria

13–12 points
Contributes little information or information lacks substance, is superficial,
  inappropriate, or irrelevant.
Speaks in single sentences or only in phrases.

GROUP INTERACTION/QUALITY OF INTERACTION

20–18 points
Is pivotal in maintaining the interaction.
Moves others through the activity.
Consistently responds to others' ideas and information.
Initiates interaction.

17–16 points
Helps maintain the interaction.
Helps move others through the activity.
Sometimes responds to others' ideas and information.
Initiates interaction.

15–14 points
Rarely helps maintain the interaction or move others through the activity.
Only role in interaction seems to be taking an appropriate turn OR
  sometimes dominates the interaction (preventing others from participating).

13–12 points
Seems to take his/her turn, but nothing else.
Does not contribute to maintaining the interaction OR definitely dominates the
  interaction.

VOCABULARY

20–18 points
Demonstrates extensive vocabulary.
No use of English words.
Almost always uses appropriate word.
Rarely if ever searches for words.

17–16 points
Demonstrates a large vocabulary.
No use of English words.
Almost always uses appropriate word.
Seldom misses or searches for words.

15–14 points
Demonstrates moderate vocabulary.
Sometimes uses English or invents words.
Frequently misses or searches for words.

13–12 points
Demonstrates small vocabulary.
Overuses English or overuses invented words.
Vocabulary limits interaction.

COMPREHENSIBILITY

20–18 points
Stays all in Spanish and comprehensibility not affected by errors.

FIGURE 9.1 *Continued.*

17–16 points
Stays all in Spanish but comprehensibility sometimes affected.

15–14 points
Sometimes uses English and/or comprehensibility is affected.

13–12 points
Overuse of English and/or comprehensibility is effortful.

GRAMMAR

20–18 points
Uses appropriate syntax and morphological forms.
Controls most structures used (consistently high performance).
Few error types.

17–16 points
Uses mostly appropriate syntax and morphological forms.
Controls some of structures used (some inconsistency in performance).
Errors are frequent.

15–14 points
Uses inappropriate syntax and morphological forms.
Control of structures is an issue.
Errors are frequent.

13–12 points
Uses inappropriate syntax and morphological forms.
Control of structures is an issue.
Errors dominate.

FIGURE 9.1 *Continued*

that in item 5, the test-takers are given the evaluation criteria. It is important that they know how they will be evaluated, especially in light of the fact that dominating an interaction is viewed and scored negatively. As you examine the criteria for evaluation, note that there are five equally weighted categories; each carries a point value of 20. Each category has four levels. If you add the points associated with the lowest possible scores, you will see that the lowest possible score is 60. In other words, a learner cannot fail the oral exam. These decisions represent only one set of possibilities. Others may decide to include other categories. Others may decide to weight the categories differently to emphasize particular aspects involved in testing oral language. Still others may decide that it is possible and desirable for someone to be able to fail the oral exam.

At Higher Levels

We now present a test section derived from a higher-level activity. Oral Test Section 12 A.3   Mentally and Physically Active requires multiple participants, and thus examines

Instructors may have practical concerns about how much time oral testing requires. To what extent should practical concerns determine instructional practices? Is the time involved so prohibitive that a communicatively oriented curriculum should exclude oral testing? Is oral testing so critical to a communicatively oriented curriculum that time should not be a factor?

the processes of communication in an ongoing manner. The test section is very nearly identical to its in-class counterpart. The intermediary steps that required reporting to the class and listening to others' reports have been removed. If Activity A.3 was not done in class, this test section will be ideal. If, on the other hand, Activity A.3 was done in class, the group of test-takers assigned to carry it out as a testing event should not have worked together in class.

Oral Test Section 12 A.3 Mentally and Physically Active *Multiple Test-Takers*

Step 1. Work together to indicate if each activity is mentally or physically active.

	MENTALLY ACTIVE	PHYSICALLY ACTIVE
1. dancing at a party	❑	❑
2. riding a bike	❑	❑
3. playing video games	❑	❑
4. playing a sport	❑	❑
5. reading a book	❑	❑
6. watching TV	❑	❑
7. writing a letter	❑	❑
8. making dinner	❑	❑
9. _____	❑	❑

Step 2. Now complete the following sentences for each of the activities listed in Step 1.

1. If dancing at a party involved _____ , then it would also involve mental activity.
2. If riding a bike involved _____ , then it would also involve _____ activity.
3. If playing video games involved _____ , then it would also involve _____ activity.
4. If playing a sport involved _____ , then it would also involve _____ activity.
5. If reading a book involved _____ , then it would also involve _____ activity.
6. If watching TV involved _____ , then it would also involve _____ activity.
7. If writing a letter involved _____ , then it would also involve _____ activity.
8. If making dinner involved _____ , then it would also involve _____ activity.
9. If _____ involved _____ , then it would also involve _____ activity.

Step 3. Decide as a group which of the following statements is true.
   a. It is easier to add mental activity to a physical one.
   b. It is easier to add physical activity to a mental one.

c. It is just as easy to add mental activity to a physical one as it is to add physical activity to a mental one.

d. Other: _____

TWO EXAMPLES OF MULTIPLE TEST-TAKERS CARRYING OUT A TASK-BASED ORAL TEST

In this section, we present transcriptions of two cases of multiple test-takers carrying out a task-based oral test. The learners in Group 1 were enrolled in first-semester Spanish, whereas the learners in Group 2 were enrolled in fourth-semester. The purpose for including the interactions of first-semester learners is to illustrate that very early-stage learners of a second language can interact with each other using a task-based format. In other words, even learners who have studied the language for approximately 10 weeks can, without an instructor's or test-giver's intervention, successfully manipulate the requirements of the activity. The purpose for including the fourth-semester learners is to provide points of both comparison and contrast. They, too, successfully manipulate the requirements of the activity without an instructor's or test-giver's intervention. In contrast, the fourth-semester learners use language differently from the first-semester learners.

The learners were given 8 minutes to prepare (Skehan & Foster 1997), during which time they worked individually. They were to read over the activity and, as they did, to think of different things they could say during each step. They were not allowed to use dictionaries or other materials during either the preparation or the testing phase. The three first-semester learners taking the oral exam were female. Two of the three fourth-semester learners were female, the other was male. The testing time allotted was 8 minutes. The testing sessions were videotaped and the transcriptions were taken from these videotapes.

Following is the activity they were given to carry out; they were asked to name the most interesting people they can think of in their Spanish class, in the United States, and in the world. They were not limited to living people but could also talk about people from the past. The original activity was written in Spanish, but is translated here for the benefit of the reader.

Oral Test Activity. The Most Interesting Person

Step 1. Prepare a list of all the words, ideas, or concepts that you associate with the word *interesting*.

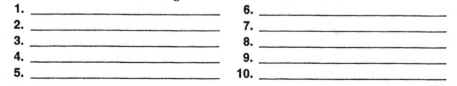

1. _____	6. _____
2. _____	7. _____
3. _____	8. _____
4. _____	9. _____
5. _____	10. _____

Step 2. Think about the most interesting person in your Spanish class. Who is it? What are his or her characteristics? What words/ideas/concepts from Step 1 apply to this person?

Step 3. Think about the most interesting person in the United States. (The person can be from the past, not only from the present.) Who is it? What are his or her characteristics? What words/ideas/concepts from Step 1 apply to this person?

Step 4. Think about the most interesting person in the world. (The person can be from the past, not only from the present.) Who is it? What are his or her characteristics? What words/ideas/concepts from Step 1 apply to this person?

As you read over the following transcript of the interaction, you might recall the definition of *conversation* presented in Chapter 2 as the "informal exchange of thoughts and feelings" (*American Heritage Dictionary* 1973, p. 291). The three learners do indeed exchange their thoughts and feelings; they converse. They respond to the things that they say to each other. All three participants speak to each other, for example, in lines 21–37 about their respective instructors, in lines 38–54 about President Clinton, in lines 55–60 about Evita Perón as played by Madonna, and in lines 68–94 about Michael Jordan. Also note the leadership role S2 assumes in this interaction. She initiates the moves to each of the steps in the activity (lines 1, 21, 38, and 55), keeps the activity going toward the allotted 8 minutes (line 68), and questions the other participants to explain themselves (lines 18, 48, and 64). Finally, you might note that the students created their own version of the activity. They did not use the associations in Step 1 to justify their choices in later steps. And they tended to provide physical descriptions of the people they nominated as interesting.

Group 1 Transcript   First-Semester learners

[The interaction took place in Spanish but is translated into English. Words spoken in English appear in italic. The translation cannot capture the quality of the learners' Spanish; there is no way to translate their incorrect gender agreement or many other concordance errors.]

1.	s2:	Hello, um. What words do you think, um, interesting?
2.	s1:	Um, comical.
3.	s3:	Nice.
4.	s2:	Adventurous.
5.	s3:	Intelligent.
6.	s1:	Extroverted, introverted.
7.	s3:	Is responsible.
8.	s1:	Responsible.
9.	s3:	Yes, and athletic.
10.	s2:	Is not shy.
11.	s3:	Is very, um . . .
12.	s1:	Tall.
13.	s1, s2, s3:	Yes.
14.	s2:	Reads a lot.
15.	s3:	Very good student.
16.	s1:	A lot . . . a lot of freckles.
17.	s3:	Um . . .
18.	s2:	Freckles are interesting?

19.	s1:	Um, a lot of freckles, is very interesting.
20.	s3:	Um, is a lot of friends is interesting. It is possible.
21.	s2:	[*Reads from activity sheet.*] Who is interesting in Spanish class?
22.	s3:	Your professor.
23.	s1:	Yes, my professor in my Spanish.
24.	s3:	We are professor is short.
25.	s1:	My professor is short. His hair is curly? But very, very interesting.
26.	s3:	Yes, he is, he is not boring.
27.	s2:	My professor is very, very cute and tall.
28.	s3:	And shoes is tall, *also.*
29.	s1:	My professor is very nice, is, um, he is very, um, interesting but ah . . .
30.	s3:	The professor has dark hair and straight.
31.	s2:	And dark eyes.
32.	s3:	Blue.
33.	s2:	Blue, yes.
34.	s3:	Yes.
35.	s1:	My professor explains directions very well, he, the class.
36.	s2:	But my professor doesn't . . .
37.	s3:	Doesn't speak English. [*Laughter.*]
38.	s2:	Ok, Step 3, please. Um, the president is the most interesting in the United States.
39.	s3:	Yes, he is intelligent.
40.	s1:	He is boring, boring.
41.	s3:	He is ugly. He is ugly.
42.	s2:	But you have a talent for leadership. [*Laughter.*]
43.	s1:	The president speaks very, very . . .
44.	s2:	Boring.
45.	s1:	Boring.
46.	s3:	He is ugly.
47.	s1:	But he is logical, [*uninterpretable word*] on television.
48.	s2:	Do you think ugly or cute?
49.	s1:	Ugly.
50.	s3:	Ugly, a lot ugly. He is, um . . .
51.	s2:	Big nose.
52.	s3:	Yes, um, red hair.
53.	s1:	He plays football in um . . .
54.	s3:	College.
55.	s2:	[*Reads from activity sheet.*] Who is the most interesting person in, in the world?
56.	s1:	Evita Perón is very, very interesting.
57.	s2:	She is Madonna in the theater. She goes . . . I go to the theater. I don't know.
58.	s1:	Madonna singer many words in the—
59.	s2:	Thought about changing in songs. She singer.
60.	s3:	To dance and to sing.
61.	s2:	But I think the Spanish professor is most interesting for all the people.

62.	s3:	Yes.

62. s3: Yes.
63. s1: Yes.
64. s2: Why?
65. s3: Not tired in Spanish class is very interesting.
66. s2: Yes.
67. s1: Very interesting. *Me too.*
68. s2: *Me too?* What, how many *more?* OK.
69. s1: The other person in the world is, is . . .
70. s3: Is Michael Jordan.
71. s1: Yes, he plays basketball.
72. s3: He is very handsome.
73. s1: For . . .
74. s2: He plays.
75. s3: He plays?
76. s2: Yes.
77. s1: For . . . the *Bulls.*
78. s2: Los toros.
79. s1: In Chicago.
80. s2: Michael Jordan has, has, um, [*Nonsensical word,* **rosado**].
81. s1: He plays basketball.
82. s3: He is, um, Michael Jordan is . . .
83. s2: He has to do exercises a lot, every day because it is necessary, um . . .
84. s1: Michael Jordan has two children.
85. s3: Two or three?
86. s1: A girl . . . and a boy.
87. s3: Two boys and a daughter.
88. s1: Three.
89. s3: He is tall, *too.*
90. s1: Wife is short.
91. s3: On television of Oprah.
92. s2: Her hair is very short and dark eyes.
93. s3: [*Nonsensical word,* **constanos.**]
94. s2: Dark, yes, um.

As you read over the transcript of the interaction of the fourth-semester learners, you may want to note that S1 is male and that S2 and S3 are female. The immediate contrast between Groups 1 and 2 is length of utterance. The fourth-semester learners speak in complete sentences and tend to speak in multiple sentences. As in Group 1, one participant, S1, takes the leadership role to initiate the steps of the activity (lines 1, 6, 10, and 15), but another one, S2, takes the role of keeping the activity going to its allotted time (line 24). Interactions that involve all three participants contributing to the conversation are more rare with Group 2, perhaps due in part to them talking about fewer people than Group 1 did. In fact, only the exchange about Mother Teresa involves all three (lines 18–23). The exchange about President Clinton marginally involves all three (lines 24–29). S2's role is to offer the question (line 24) and to affirm a statement (line 26). The interaction principally involves S1 and S3.

[The interaction took place in Spanish but is translated into English. Words spoken in English appear in italic. The translation cannot capture the quality of the learners' Spanish; there is no way to translate their gender agreement and other concordance errors.]

1. s1: I believe that some words are intelligent, or different, or unique. What do you think?
2. s2: I think that an interesting person is not boring.
3. s3: I associate the word interesting with entertaining.
4. s2: Yes.
5. s1: Yes.
6. s1: I think that the most interesting person in our class is the girl that [*uninterpretable word*, **stive**] in *Seville* in 96 in the past.
7. s2: Oh, yes, Kristen.
8. s1: Yes, Kristen.
9. s2: I think that the most interesting person in our class is Miguel because he talks a lot and always late to class.
10. s1: I believe that the most interesting person in the United States is, ah, the Tiger Woods because he has a lot for kids to teach. He is, ah, he is multinational and he plays golf much good, very good.
11. s3: One other person also is Franklin. He has many interests . . . and . . . um, they have done many things and he wrote, and um, was in the government.
12. s2: There are many interesting people in the United States. *Let's see.* I think that government officials is very interesting. Um, and the, um, religious officials because um, you have a lot of influences, um, on the people of our country.
13. s3: Yes, on families, too.
14. s2: Yes.
15. s1: The most interesting person in the world. I don't know. There are many, many people that, um, that they have, um, a lot of influences on the world, on our world. I believe, for example, the Princess Diana. She was a person most important from the third world with . . . *societies.*
16. s2: I don't know.
17. s3: In the past Eva Perón of Argentina was very interesting and, um, the movie Evita, um, described her influence.
18. s2: I think that a person very interesting in the world is Mother Teresa. She does a lot for very many persons. She is very nice and she wins the *Nobel Peace Prize.*
19. s1: Yes, She helps like all the people of the world. The rich, the
20. s2: Poor.
21. s1: Poor.
22. s3: She had a long life.
23. s2: Yes.
24. s2: Are there other interesting people?
25. s1: I believe that the president of the United States because, ah, United States is the, the number one in the world.

26. s2: Yes.

27. s3: And his daughter is in university like us and it is interesting that the president has a family.

28. s1: Yes, past presidents all have, all not have some sons or daughters. It is a different.

29. s3: Our country has many interesting people and from many . . .

SUMMARY

In this chapter, we derived oral tests from task-based classroom activities. Three types of oral tests were presented. The first format was the most traditional in that the test-giver required the test-taker to simply report on the results of an in-class activity. The test-giver did not engage the test-taker on any other communicative dimension. The second oral test type required that the test-taker and test-giver carry out an activity together. Test-giver and test-taker shared the communicative burden of initiating and maintaining interaction. Finally, a group testing format was given. That is, test sections were developed in which multiple test-takers carried out a task-based activity. Issues also surround these approaches to oral testing, including presence of bias in the test-giver, appropriate scoring criteria, and rewarding appropriate learner behavior. These issues are not insurmountable, and suggestions were offered to address them. Furthermore, oral exam procedures and evaluation criteria were presented to illustrate how to bring together the concepts presented in the chapter. Finally, transcriptions of first- and fourth-semester learners carrying out a task-based oral exam were presented. These transcripts show both similarities and differences. Perhaps of greatest importance was to show that first-semester learners can successfully carry out an oral exam that does not require the direct intervention of a test-giver.

To say that something is coherent is to say that it is marked by an orderly or logical relation of parts that affords comprehension or recognition. To the extent that teaching and testing are an entwined enterprise, they should be marked by a logical relation of parts. We have attempted to provide a coherent picture of teaching and testing by deriving test sections from the activities presented in earlier chapters, bringing this presentation full circle.

GAINING GREATER PERSPECTIVE

1. *Test-Takers Respond.* Cohen (1984) and Shohamy (1982) investigated and documented test-takers' responses to a testing situation. Cohen offers us the test-takers' strategies, while Shohamy reveals the affective impact tests can have on language learners.

2. *Suggestions.* Although not a lengthy treatment of assessment, Ur (1996, pp. 244–246) provides ideas on assessment from a perspective parallel to that presented in this chapter. She states, "the type of evaluation involved here is sometimes called 'formative,' since its main purpose is to 'form': to enhance, not conclude, a process" (p. 244).

APPLICATION ACTIVITIES

1. Develop oral tests in which learners report the content of the interaction for the following.
   a. Activities A.2 and A.3 (Chapter 6)
   b. Activity Bilingualism and Biculturalism (Chapter 4)
   c. The higher-level versions of Activity B.1 (if you developed them as part of the Application Activities in Chapter 6)
2. Develop oral tests that require the test-giver and test-taker to be partners in the interaction for the following.
   a. Activities A.1, A.2, and A.3 (Chapters 3 and 6)
   b. Activity Bilingualism and Biculturalism (Chapter 4)
   c. The higher-level versions of Activity B.1 (if you developed them as part of the Application Activities in Chapter 6)
3. Develop oral test sections of Activities A.1, A.2, and B.1 that require multiple participants.
4. Create scoring criteria that you would use for each of the following testing situations. Are the criteria the same? Are the point values the same across all interactional patterns?
   a. Test-taker reports content of in-class interaction
   b. Test-taker and test-giver are partners in an interaction
   c. Multiple test-takers complete an activity
5. Use the sample criteria for evaluating oral test performance (page 138) to evaluate the six learners whose interactions are presented in the section Two Examples of Multiple Test-Takers Carrying Out a Task-Based Oral Exam. Compare your evaluations to those of others. Can you come to an agreement?
6. Examine the transcripts of the six learners in the section Two Examples of Multiple Test-Takers Carrying Out a Task-Based Oral Exam. Identify the places in which they negotiate meaning via confirmation checks, clarifications requests, paraphrases, and repetitions.

References

Allwright, D., & Bailey, K. M. (1991). *Focus on the language classroom: An introduction to classroom research for language teachers.* Cambridge: Cambridge University Press.

Bachman, L. F. (1990). *Fundamental considerations in language testing.* Oxford: Oxford University Press.

Bachman, L. F., & Palmer, A. S. (1983). *Oral test of communicative proficiency in English.* Urbana, IL: Photo-offset.

Ballman, T. L. (1996). Integrating vocabulary, grammar and culture: A model five-day communicative lesson plan. *Foreign Language Annals, 29,* 37–44.

Belleck, A. A., Kliebard, H., Hyman, R., & Smith, F. (1966). *The language of the classroom.* New York: Teachers College Press.

Beretta, A. (1987). The Bangalore project: Description and evaluation. In S. Savignon & M. Bernes (Eds.), *Initiatives in communicative language teaching II,* pp. 83–106. Reading, MA: Addison Wesley Longman.

Bernhardt, E. B. (1992). *Reading development in a second language.* Norwood, NJ: Ablex.

Breen, M. (1987). Learner contributions to task design. In C. Candlin & D. Murphy (Eds.), *Language learning tasks* (pp. 23–46). Englewood Cliffs, NJ: Prentice Hall.

Breen, M., & Candlin, C. (1979). Essentials of a communicative curriculum in language teaching. *Applied Linguistics, 1,* 90–112.

Brindley, G. (1987). Factors affecting task difficulty. In D. Nunan (Ed.), *Guidelines for the development of curriculum resources.* Adelaide, Australia: National Curriculum Resource Center.

Brooks, F. B. (1990). Foreign language learning: A social interaction perspective. In B. VanPatten & J. F. Lee (Eds.), *Second language acquisition—foreign language learning: Perspectives on research and practice,* pp. 153–169. Clevedon, UK: Multilingual Matters.

Brooks, F. B. (1992). Can we talk? *Foreign Language Annals, 25,* 59–71.

Brooks, F. B. (1993). Some problems and caveats in "communicative" discourse: Toward a conceptualization of the foreign language classroom. *Foreign Language Annals, 26,* 233–242.

Brooks, F. B., & Donato, R. (1994). Vygotskyan approaches to understanding foreign language learner discourse during communicative tasks. *Hispania, 77,* 262–274.

Brooks, F. B., Donato, R., & McGlone, J. V. (1997). When are they going to say "it" right? Understanding learner talk during pair-work activity. *Foreign Language Annals, 40,* 524–541.

Brown, G., & Yule, G. (1983). *Discourse analysis.* Cambridge: Cambridge University Press.

Brown, H. D. (1987). *Principles of language learning and teaching,* 2nd ed. Englewood Cliffs, NJ: Prentice Hall.

Brown, J., & Palmer, A. (1988). *The listening approach: Methods and materials for applying Krashen's input hypothesis.* New York: Longman.

Byrnes, H. (1991). Reflections on the development of cross-cultural competence in the foreign language classroom. In B. Freed (Ed.), *Foreign language acquisition research and the classroom* (pp. 205–218). Lexington, MA: D. C. Heath.

Canale, M. (1983). From communicative competence to communicative language pedagogy. In J. Richards & R. Schmidt (Eds.), *Language and communication*. London: Longman.

Canale, M., & Swain, M. (1980). Theoretical bases of communicative approaches to second language teaching and testing. *Applied Linguistics, 1*, 1–47.

Candlin, C. (1987). Toward task-based learning. In C. Candlin & D. Murphy (Eds.), *Language learning tasks*, pp. 5–22. Englewood Cliffs, NJ: Prentice Hall.

Candlin, C., & Murphy, D. (Eds.), *Language learning tasks*. Englewood Cliffs, NJ: Prentice Hall.

Carroll, J. B. (1980). *Testing communicative performance*. London: Pergamon.

Cazden, C. B. (1986). Classroom discourse. In M. C. Wittrock (Ed.), *Handbook of research on teaching*, pp. 432–463. New York: Macmillan.

Chastain, K., & Guntermann, G. (1987). *Imagínate: Managing Spanish Conversations*. Boston: Heinle & Heinle.

Cohen, A. D. (1984). On taking tests: What the students report. *Language Testing, 1*, 70–81.

Coleman, H. (1987). 'Little tasks make large return': Task-based language learning in large crowds. In C. Candlin & D. Murphy (Eds.), *Language learning tasks*, pp. 121–146. Englewood Cliffs, NJ: Prentice Hall.

Cook, V. (1991). *Second language learning and language teaching*. New York: Edward Arnold.

Coughlan, P., & Duff, P. (1994). Same task: Different activities: Analysis of a SLA task from an activity theory perspective. In J. Lantolf & G. Appel (Eds.), *Vygotskyan approaches to second language research*, pp. 173–193. Norwood, NJ: Ablex.

Crookes, G., & Gass, S. M. (Eds.) (1993a). *Tasks and language learning: Integrating theory and practice*. Clevedon, UK: Multilingual Matters.

Crookes, G., & Gass, S. M. (Eds.) (1993b). *Tasks in a pedagogical context: Integrating theory and practice*. Clevedon, UK: Multilingual Matters.

Daly, J. (1991). Understanding communication apprehension: An introduction for language educators. In E. Horwitz & D. Young (Eds.), *Language anxiety: From theory and research to classroom implications*, pp. 3–14. Englewood Cliffs, NJ: Prentice Hall.

Day, R. (Ed.) (1986). *Talking to learn: Conversations and second language acquisition*. Rowley, MA: Newbury House.

Di Pietro, R. J. (1987). *Strategic interaction: Learning languages through scenarios*. Cambridge: Cambridge University Press.

Donato, R. (1994). Collective scaffolding in second language learning. In J. Lantolf & G. Appel (Eds.), *Vygotskyan approaches to second language research*, pp. 33–56. Norwood, NJ: Ablex.

Doughty, C., & Pica, T. (1986). Information gap tasks: Do they facilitate acquisition? *TESOL Quarterly, 20*, 305–326.

Ellis, R. (1990). *Instructed second language acquisition*. Oxford: Blackwell.

Finkel, D., & Monk, G. S. (1983). Teachers and learning groups: Dissolution of the Atlas complex. In C. Bouton & R. Y. Grath (Eds.), *Learning in groups*, pp. 83–97. San Francisco: Jossey-Bass.

Foley, J. (1991). A psycholinguistic framework for task-based approaches to language teaching. *Applied Linguistics, 12*, 62–75.

Fotos, S., & Ellis, R. (1991). Communicating about grammar: A task-based approach. *TESOL Quarterly, 25*, 605–629.

Freeman, D. (1992). Collaboration: Constructing shared understandings in a second language classroom. In D. Nunan (Ed.), *Collaborative language learning and teaching*, pp. 56–80. Cambridge: Cambridge University Press.

Galloway, V., & LaBarca, A. (1993). *Visión y voz*. Boston: Heinle & Heinle.

Gass, S. M., & Selinker, L. (1994). *Second language acquisition: An introductory course.* Hillsdale, NJ: Lawrence Erlbaum.

Gerngroß, G., & Puchta, H. (1984). Beyond notions and functions: Language teaching or the art of letting go. In S. Savignon & M. Berns, (Eds.), *Initiatives in communicative language teaching,* pp. 89–107. Reading, MA: Addison Wesley Longman.

Glass, W. R. (1996). Personal communication, letter.

Grice, H. P. (1975). Logic and conversation. In P. Cole & J. Morgan (Eds.), *Syntax and semantics volume 3: Speech acts,* pp. 41–58. New York: Academic Press.

Horwitz, E., & Young, D. (1991). *Language anxiety: From theory and research to classroom implications.* Englewood Cliffs, NJ: Prentice Hall.

Johnson, K. E. (1995). *Understanding communication in second language classrooms.* Cambridge: Cambridge University Press.

Kinginger, C. (1990). *Task variation and classroom learner discourse.* Unpublished doctoral dissertation. Urbana, IL: University of Illinois, Urbana-Champaign.

Kinginger, C. (1995). Toward a reflective practice of TA education. In C. Kramsch (Ed.), *Redrawing the boundaries of foreign language study,* pp. 121–140. Boston: Heinle & Heinle.

Kinginger, C. (1996). Personal communication, letter.

Koch, A., & Terrell, T. (1991). Affective reactions of foreign language students to Natural Approach activities and teaching techniques. In E. Horwitz & D. Young (Eds.), *Language anxiety: From theory and research to classroom implications,* pp. 109–126. Englewood Cliffs, NJ: Prentice Hall.

Kramsch, C. (1991). The order of discourse in language teaching. In B. Freed (Ed.), *Foreign language acquisition research and the classroom,* pp. 191–204. Lexington, MA: D. C. Heath.

Kramsch, C. (1993). *Context and culture in language teaching.* Oxford: Oxford University Press.

Krashen, S. D., & Terrell, T. D. (1983). *The natural approach.* New York: Pergamon.

Lantolf, J., & Appel, G. (Eds.) (1994). *Vygotskyan approaches to second language research.* Norwood, NJ: Ablex.

Lee, J. F. (1986). Background knowledge and L2 reading. *Modern Language Journal, 70,* 350–354.

Lee, J. F. (1987). Comprehending the Spanish subjunctive: An information processing perspective. *Modern Language Journal, 71,* 50–57.

Lee, J. F. (1989). *A manual and practical guide to directing foreign language programs and TA training.* New York: Random House.

Lee, J. F. (1995). Using task-based activities to restructure class discussions. *Foreign Language Annals, 28,* 437–446.

Lee, J. F., & Paulson, D. (1996). Writing and compositions. In B. VanPatten (Ed.), *Instructor's Manual, Testing Program, and Video Guide to accompany ¿Sabías que... ? Beginning Spanish,* 2nd ed., pp. 30–34. New York: McGraw-Hill.

Lee, J. F., Wolf, D. F., Young, D. J., & Chandler, P. M. (1996). *¿Qué te parece? Intermediate Spanish.* New York: McGraw-Hill.

Lee, J. F., & VanPatten, B. (1995). *Making communicative language teaching happen.* New York: McGraw-Hill.

Lee, J. F., Binkowski, A., & VanPatten, B. (1994). *Ideas: Estrategias, lecturas, actividades y composiciones.* New York: McGraw-Hill.

Legutke, M., & Thomas, H. (1991). *Process and experience in the language classroom.* New York: Longman.

Leeman Guthrie, E. (1984). Intake, communication and second language teaching. In S. J. Savignon & M. Berns (Eds.), *Initiatives in communicative language teaching,* pp. 35–54. Reading, MA: Addison Wesley Longman.

Lightbown, P., & Spada, N. (1993). *How languages are learned.* Oxford: Oxford University Press.

Littlejohn, A., & Hicks, D. (1987). Task-centered writing activities. In C. Candlin & D. Murphy (Eds.), *Language learning tasks,* pp. 69–92. Englewood Cliffs, NJ: Prentice Hall.

Long, M. (1983). Linguistics and conversational adjustments to nonnative speakers. *Studies in Second Language Acquisition, 5,* 177–193.

Long, M. (1985). A role for instruction in second language acquisition. Task-based language training. In K. Hyltenstam & M. Pienemann (Eds.), *Modelling and assessing second language acquisition,* pp. 77–99. Clevedon, UK: Multilingual Matters.

Lowe, P. (1982). *Manual for FS oral interview workshop.* Washington, DC: DLA/FS Joint Oral Interview Transfer Project.

Mackey, A. (1995). *Stepping up the pace: Input, interaction and interlanguage development. An empirical study of questions in ESL.* Unpublished Ph.D. dissertation, University of Sydney.

Maley, A. (1984). "I got religion"—evangelism in language teaching. In S. Savignon & M. Berns (Eds.), *Initiatives in communicative language teaching,* pp. 79–86. Reading, MA: Addison Wesley Longman.

Mehan, H. (1979). *Learning lessons: Social organization in the classroom.* Cambridge, MA: Harvard University Press.

Moskowitz, G. (1978). *Caring and sharing in the foreign language classroom.* Rowley, MA: Newbury House.

Musumeci, D. (1997). *Breaking tradition: An exploration of the historical relationship between theory and practice in second language teaching.* New York: McGraw-Hill.

Nunan, D. (1989). *Designing tasks for the communicative classroom.* Cambridge: Cambridge University Press.

Nunan, D. (1991). Communicative tasks and the language curriculum. *TESOL Quarterly, 25,* 279–295.

Omaggio, A. C. (1986). *Language teaching in context: Proficiency-oriented instruction.* Boston: Heinle & Heinle.

Omaggio Hadley, A. (1993). *Language teaching in context.* Boston: Heinle & Heinle.

Paulston, C. B. (1978). Structural pattern drills: A classification. In E. G. Joiner & P. B. Westphal (Eds.), *Developing communication skills: General considerations and specific techniques,* pp. 21–31. Rowley, MA: Newbury House.

Pica, T. (1992). The textual outcomes of native speaker–non-native speaker negotiation: What do they reveal about second language learning? In C. Kramsch & S. McConnell-Ginet (Eds.), *Text and context: Cross-disciplinary perspectives on language study,* pp. 198–237. Lexington, MA: D. C. Heath.

Pica, T., Kanagy, R., & Falodun, J. (1993). Choosing and using communication tasks for second language research and instruction. In G. Crookes & S. Gass (Eds.), *Tasks and language learning: Integrating theory and practice,* pp. 9–34. Clevedon, UK: Multilingual Matters.

Porter, P. A. (1986). How learners talk to each other: Input and interaction in task-centered discussions. In R. Day (Ed.), *Talking to learn: Conversation in second language acquisition,* pp. 200–224. Rowley, MA: Newbury House.

Prabhu, N. (1987). *Second language pedagogy: A perspective.* Oxford: Oxford University Press.

Rea Dickins, P. M., & Woods, E. G. (1988). Some criteria for the development of communicative grammar tasks. *TESOL Quarterly, 22,* 623–646.

Richard-Amato, P. (1988). *Making it happen: Interaction in the second language classroom.* New York: Longman.

Richards, J., Platt, J., & Weber, H. (1985). *Longman Dictionary of Applied Linguistics*. New York: Longman.

Richards, J., & Lockhart, C. (1994). *Reflective teaching in second language classrooms*. Cambridge: Cambridge University Press.

Richards, J., & Rogers, T. (1986). *Approaches and methods in language teaching*. Cambridge: Cambridge University Press.

Riley, G., & Lee, J. F. (1996). A comparison of summary and recall protocols as measures of second language reading comprehension. *Language Testing, 13*, 173–187.

Rivers, W. (1972). *Speaking in many tongues*. Rowley, MA: Newbury House.

Rulon, K. A., & McCreary, J. (1986). Negotiation of content: Teacher-fronted and small-group interaction. In R. Day (Ed.), *Talking to learn: Conversation in second language acquisition*, pp. 182–199. Rowley, MA: Newbury House.

Sadow, S. (1982). *Idea bank*. Cambridge, MA: Newbury House.

Savignon, S. J. (1972). *Communicative competence: An experiment in foreign language teaching*. Philadelphia, PA: Center for Curriculum Development.

Savignon, S. J. (1983). *Communicative competence: Theory and classroom practice: Texts and contexts in second language learning*. Reading, MA: Addison Wesley Longman.

Savignon, S. J. (1997). *Communicative competence: Theory and classroom practice: Texts and contexts in second language learning*, 2nd ed. New York: McGraw-Hill.

Schön, D. (1983). *The reflective practitioner: How professionals think in action*. New York: Basic Books.

Shohamy, E. (1982). Affective considerations in language testing. *Modern Language Journal, 66*, 13–17.

Shohamy, E. (1984). Does the testing method make a difference? The case of reading comprehension. *Language Testing, 1*, 147–170.

Shohamy, E. (1993). The power of tests: The impact of language tests on teaching and learning. *National Foreign Language Center Occasional Papers* (June).

Shohamy, E., Reves, T., & Bejerano, Y. (1986). Introducing a new comprehensive test of oral proficiency. *English Language Teaching Journal, 40*, 212–222.

Shrum, J. L., & Glisan, E. W. (1994). *Teacher's handbook: Contextualized language instruction*. Boston: Heinle & Heinle.

Sinclair, J., & Coulthard, R. (1975). *Towards an analysis of discourse: The English used by teachers and pupils*. London: Oxford University Press.

Skehan, P., & Foster, P. (1997). Task type and task processing conditions as influences on foreign language performance. *Language Teaching Research, 1*, 185–211.

Swaffar, J. K. (1992). Written texts and cultural readings. In C. J. Kramsch & S. McConnell-Ginet (Eds.), *Text and context: Cross-disciplinary perspectives on language study*, pp. 238–250. Lexington, MA: D. C. Heath.

Swaffar, J. K., Arens, K., & Byrnes, H. (1991). *Reading for meaning: An integrated approach to foreign language learning*. Englewood Cliffs, NJ: Prentice Hall.

Swain, M. (1985). Communicative competence: Some roles of comprehensible input and comprehensible output in its development. In S. M. Gass & C. Madden (Eds.), *Input in second language acquisition*, pp. 235–253. Rowley, MA: Newbury House.

Tarnone, E. (1984). Teaching strategic competence in the foreign language classroom. In S. J. Savignon & M. S. Berns (Eds.), *Initiatives in communicative language teaching*, pp. 127–136. Reading, MA: Addison Wesley Longman.

Terrell, T. D. (1986). Acquisition in the Natural Approach: The binding/access framework. *Modern Language Journal, 70*, 213–227.

Terrell, T. D. (1991). The role of grammar instruction in a communicative approach. *Modern Language Journal, 75*, 52–63.

Ur, P. (1996). *A course in language teaching: Theory and practice*. Cambridge: Cambridge University Press.

Valdman, A. (1992). Authenticity, variation, and communication in the foreign language classroom. In C. J. Kramsch & S. McConnell-Ginet (Eds.), *Text and context: Cross-disciplinary perspectives on language study*, pp. 79–97. Lexington, MA: D. C. Heath.

Van Lier, L. (1991). Inside the classroom: Teaching procedures and learning processes. *Applied Language Learning, 2*, 29–68.

VanPatten, B. (1987). On babies and bathwater: Input in foreign language learning. *Modern Language Journal, 71*, 154–164.

VanPatten, B. (1988). How juries get hung: Problems with the evidence for a focus on form. *Language Learning, 38*, 243–260.

VanPatten, B. (1991). The foreign language classroom as a place to communicate. In B. Freed (Ed.), *Foreign language acquisition research and the classroom*, pp. 54–73. Lexington, MA: D. C. Heath.

VanPatten, B. (1993). Grammar teaching for the acquisition-rich classroom. *Foreign Language Annals, 26*, 435–450.

VanPatten, B. (1996). *Input processing and grammar instruction: Theory, research, challenges and implications*. Norwood, NJ: Ablex.

VanPatten, B., & Cadierno, T. (1993). Explicit instruction and input processing. *Studies in Second Language Acquisition, 15*, 225–243.

VanPatten, B., Lee. J. F., Ballman, T. L., & Dvorak, T. (1992). *¿Sabías que... ? Beginning Spanish*. New York: McGraw-Hill.

VanPatten, B., Lee. J. F., & Ballman, T. L. (1996). *¿Sabías que... ? Beginning Spanish*, 2nd ed. New York: McGraw-Hill.

Varonis, E., & Gass, S. (1985). Non-native/non-native conversations: A model for negotiation of meaning. *Applied Linguistics, 6*, 71–90.

Vygotsky, L. (1978). *Mind in society*. Cambridge, MA: Harvard University Press.

Wallace, M. (1991). *Training foreign language teachers: A reflective approach*. Cambridge: Cambridge University Press.

Wilkinson, L. (1982). Introduction: A sociolinguistic approach to communicating in the classroom. In L. Wilkinson (Ed.), *Communicating in the classroom*, pp. 3–12. New York: Academic Press.

Wright, A., Betteridge, D., & Buckby, M. (1984). *Games for language learning*. Cambridge: Cambridge University Press.

Wright, T. (1987). Instructional task and discoursal outcome in the L2 classroom. In C. Candlin & D. Murphy (Eds.), *Language learning tasks*, pp. 47–68. Englewood Cliffs, NJ: Prentice Hall.

Wolf, D. F. (1993a). Issues in reading comprehension assessment: Implications for the development of research instruments and classroom tests. *Foreign Language Annals, 26*, 322–331.

Wolf, D. F. (1993b). A comparison of assessment tasks used to measure foreign language reading comprehension. *Modern Language Journal, 77*, 473–488.

Young, D. (1991). The relationship between anxiety and foreign language oral proficiency ratings. In E. Horwitz & D. Young (Eds.), *Language anxiety: From theory and research to classroom implications*, pp. 57–64. Englewood Cliffs, NJ: Prentice Hall.

Young, D. (1999). *Affect in foreign language and second language learning: A practical guide to creating a low-anxiety classroom atmosphere*. New York: McGraw-Hill.

Index

Note: Page numbers followed by *f* indicate figures; those followed by *t* indicate tables.

About the Author

James F. Lee is Associate Professor of Spanish, Director of Language Instruction, and Director of the Programs in Hispanic Linguistics in the Department of Spanish and Portuguese at Indiana University. He serves on the editorial board of Spanish Applied Linguistics, and, with Bill VanPatten, serves as General Editor of the McGraw-Hill Second Language Professional Series.

His research interests lie in the areas of second language reading comprehension, input processing, and exploring the relationship between the two. His work has appeared in such journals as *Studies in Second Language Acquisition, The Modern Language Journal, Applied Language Learning,* and *Spanish Applied Linguistics.* His previous publications include *Making Communicative Language Teaching Happen,* co-authored with Bill VanPatten, and several co-edited volumes: *Foreign Language Learning: A Research Perspective, Second Language Acquisition-Foreign Language Learning,* and *Language and Language Use: Studies in Spanish.* He and Albert Valdman are currently preparing *Multiple Perspectives on Form and Meaning,* the 1999 volume of the American Association of University Supervisors and Coordinators. Additionally, he has co-authored several Spanish-language textbooks, including *¿Qué te parece? Intermediate Spanish, ¿Sabías que...? Beginning Spanish,* and *Ideas: Estrategias, lecturas, actividades y composiciones.*